Endorsements

...

You've probably heard the statement "To God be the glory!" The word glory means adoring praise and worshipful thanksgiving; a sense of wonder and elation. As I read this book proclaiming the rich history of ministry in Kansas City, I felt the glory of God (His presence), experienced the glory from God (His power), and I give glory to God (His praise). May all who read this book shout, "To God be the glory!!"

- Rod Handley, Founder & President, Character that Counts

The Spiritual Roots of Kansas City is a fascinating exploration of our city's history and heritage! The book unfolds how from the time of Lewis and Clark's exploration to the arrival of French settlers and prayerful missionaries, our city was shaped and founded on diversity and faith. Through the depression era on into the civil rights Freedom marches of the 60s and then into the youth movement of the 70s and 80s, faith in action continued to be a hallmark of our city. Read Bill and Annika's wonderful work – you will find God's fingerprints in our past and inspiration for His work in the future!

- Mike Bickley, Lead Pastor, Journey Bible Church

God is always at work. In the hectic pace of our lives, it is easy for us to fail to see his hand in all things, and important that we take times to stop and take note of all that he has done. Bill and Annika have provided the church of Kansas City a historical treasure by providing a record of the amazing work that God has accomplished in our midst. To God be the Glory! I believe he wants to do greater things in the days to come.

- Matt Adams, Pastor of Community Impact, Westside Family Church

The story of the Church in Kansas City is a story that must be told. This book navigates us through the tumultuous journey that led to what we see today as the Body of Christ in our metro area. What you see is one God story after the next. A troublesome yet seamless orchestration of circumstance and the will of God causing all things to work together for the good of the Church. I praise God that this work has been finally documented for all to share in this testimony.

- Greg Ealey, Campus Pastor, Colonial Presbyterian Church South KC; and Executive Director, Elevate KC

Bill High and Annika Bergen deftly navigate the Church's history within Kansas City. This book is highly recommended for anyone wishing to delve into the rich history of Christianity in this region.

- Zach Daughtrey, Historian, Kansas City Catholic Diocese

THE SPIRITUAL ROOTS
of
Kansas City

Discovering the Past to Shape Our Future

BILL HIGH AND **ANNIKA BERGEN**

The Spiritual Roots of Kansas City.

© 2019 Bill High, Annika Bergen. All rights reserved. No part of this book may be reproduced in any form or by any electronic or mechanical means including information storage or by any retrieval systems, except for brief quotations in printed reviews, without prior permission in writing from the authors.

Scripture quotations marked ESV are from The ESV® Bible (The Holy Bible, English Standard Version®), copyright © 2001 by Crossway, a publishing ministry of Good News Publishers. Used by permission. All rights reserved.

Scripture quotations marked NIV are taken from the Holy Bible, New International Version®, NIV®. Copyright © 1973, 1978, 1984, 2011 by Biblica, Inc.™ Used by permission of Zondervan. All rights reserved worldwide. www.Zondervan.com. The "NIV" and "New International Version" are trademarks registered in the United States Patent and Trademark Office by Biblica, Inc.™

Scripture quotations marked NLT are taken from the Holy Bible, New Living Translation, copyright ©1996, 2004, 2015 by Tyndale House Foundation. Used by permission of Tyndale House Publishers, Inc., Carol Stream, Illinois 60188.

All rights reserved.

Cover and interior design by Justin Park.

To the board of The Signatry:

• • •

*Thank you for believing in Kansas City,
that our city might be a light on a hill,
for loving and relying on Jesus,
and for giving your lives
in service of both.*

Those who are wise will take all this to heart; they will see in our history the faithful love of the LORD.

Psalm 107:43, NLT

• • •

. . . for I have many in this city who are my people.

Acts 18:10, ESV

• • •

He turns a desert into pools of water, a parched land into springs of water. And there he lets the hungry dwell, and they establish a city to live in; they sow fields and plant vineyards and get a fruitful yield. By his blessing they multiply greatly, and he does not let their livestock diminish.

Psalm 107:35-38, ESV

Contents

Acknowledgments 7
Preface 8
How to Read This Book 11

Chapter 1 - Fur Traders and Missionaries (1804 – 1850) 15
Chapter 2 - A Faulty Auction and a Flood (1838 – 1860) 29
Chapter 3 - The Civil War Splits the Church (1850 – 1870) 41
Chapter 4 - Growth through Diversity (1869 – 1915) 53
Chapter 5 - Dreamers Build the City (1880 – 1921) 65
Chapter 6 - Mobsters and Madams (1900 – 1939) 85
Chapter 7 - Seeds of Change (1910 – 1965) 101
Chapter 8 - Taking Back the Youth (1940 – 1980) 115
Chapter 9 - Freedom Marches and Riots (1968) 131
Chapter 10 - A New Millennium of Growth (1984 – 2019) ...141
Epilogue 153

Resources:
God's Plan for Cities 157
Small Group Discussion Guide 163
Timeline 187

Bibliography 195

Acknowledgments

• • •

We stand on the shoulders of so many who have made this book possible. We would like to specifically thank . . .

Those who happily participated in interviews as we wrote the modern history of an era never before recorded:
- Mike Bickle, director of the International House of Prayer of Kansas City
- Rick Boxx, founder and CEO of Unconventional Business Network
- Nathaniel Bozarth, anthropologist and media producer
- Zach Daughtrey, historian for the Catholic Diocese of Kansas City-St. Joseph
- David Davies, gift planning advisor for Wycliffe Bible Translators
- Dr. Greg Ealey, campus pastor at Colonial Presbyterian Church
- Marilyn Griffin, director of Ministries of New Life
- Rod Handley, founder and president of Character That Counts
- Dr. Robert Hill, former pastor of Community Christian Church
- Gary Kendall, director of Love KC
- Mike King, director of Youthfront
- Bob Lehleitner, pastor of discipleship at Colonial Presbyterian Church
- Craig McElvain, executive director of Regional Evangelical Alliance of Churches
- Shanna Steitz, pastor of Community Christian Church

Those who provided valuable feedback, encouragement, and guidance for the book:
- Gary Ascanio, broker at VantagePointe Financial Group
- Emmitt Mitchell, president of the Moody Center
- Gary Schmitz, director of the Citywide Prayer Movement

Rebecca Wright for helping compile photos.

Michael Wells, Missouri Valley Special Collections Librarian, for going above and beyond in researching historic photos.

Those who provided photos and do an excellent job preserving our local history:
Catholic Diocese of Kansas City-St. Joseph, Jackson County Historical Society, Johnson County Museum, Kansas City Museum, Kansas State Historical Society, and UMKC Special Collections.

Every church member in Kansas City, past and present—your lives have written the material in this book. Thank you.

Preface
...

Discovering My City

I (Bill) was five years old when my parents drove me to downtown Kansas City. They had an errand to run, and I was an unwilling participant. From my backseat window and my five-year-old mind, I peered at the towering skyscrapers. I wasn't impressed.

It was another twenty years before I would spend much time again in the heart of the city. I was a young lawyer and found myself sitting in an office in one of those skyscrapers. I appreciated the view and the proximity to lots of restaurants, but my appreciation was still only inches deep. Not too many years later through a long, circuitous path, I found myself volunteering in urban ministry. For the first time, I was exposed to some of the darkest parts of the city. Crime. Filth. Prostitution. Trafficking. Abuses I could not even put a name to.

But as I labored, I found great soldiers, warriors really, who gave their lives, literally, to bring light and unity to those dark places. Their sacrifices raised in me a wonder of why they would give their lives for this place they called home.

My journeys began stirring in me some of my first questions of God's purpose for cities. Why did he make them? Do cities have their own unique destiny? And what of the people who had gone before me? Why do we have streets named after people that I don't even know? These questions set me on a path of exploration into the history of my city. Perhaps God had a design for Kansas City?

The Bible and Cities

My journey also caused me to look at Scripture anew concerning cities. For instance, do you know the first city in the Bible? After Cain killed his brother, he ran from the presence of God to the land of Nod, which means wandering. There, he established the city of Enoch, which he named after his son. Some cities are bad, like Sodom and Gomorrah. Or consider Jericho—it was considered bad enough that it was cursed. Joshua said that anyone who would rebuild Jericho would do so "at the cost of his firstborn . . . and of his youngest son." Some cities were good. In Revelation 21:2, Jerusalem is described as the Holy City.

Not surprisingly, cities have a particular character about them. They stand for something. Bethlehem, which means house of bread, was where Ruth met Boaz, David was a shepherd, and Jesus was born. As Jesus nears the point of His crucifixion, he specifically prays with great emotion over Jerusalem:

• • •

"O Jerusalem, Jerusalem, the city that kills the prophets and stones those who are sent to it! How often would I have gathered your children together as a hen gathers her brood under her wings, and you were not willing!" (Matthew 23:37, ESV)

• • •

God cares about cities. In the book of Jonah, the city of Nineveh repents after hearing the prophet's message of impending destruction. Jonah complains about God's mercy, and God responds with a rhetorical question: "Should I not be concerned about that great city?"

All of these thoughts raised in me questions about my city. What are the spiritual roots of Kansas City? What had been the work of God in times past?

The Prophetic City

I found a book which helped me in my quest. Nearly one hundred years ago, in 1928, Charles P. Deatherage wrote *Early History of Greater Kansas City: The Prophetic City at the Mouth of the Kaw* (that is, the Kansas River). Here's what is amazing about Deatherage's work: He refers to Kansas City as "the prophetic and magnificent city at the Mouth of the Kaw." Why was our city prophetic?

Kansas City pride ran high in 1928. Deatherage wrote his history two years after the Liberty Memorial opened—the only World War I memorial in the country. Even President Coolidge attended the dedication ceremony. It makes sense that Kansas Citians referred to their city as the "magnificent city," with their accomplishments being recognized nationwide. But prophetic?

Deatherage's introduction references a legend about Senator Thomas H. Benton, stating that in the 1840s and 1850s—a few years after Kansas City (then "the Town of Kansas") began—he prophesied that it would become "a great commercial center." Looking back we can see that his prophecy came true. But we can also see that the name "the prophetic city" may have been an even more appropriate title for Kansas City than either the senator or the historian ever imagined.

Kansas City has always been a beacon of light for Christianity. Missionaries and Catholics settled the area. Jesuit priests followed after them and founded the first church. Then came the revivals, where thousands rallied around D.L. Moody, Billy Sunday, or Billy Graham. Thousands more came to Christ during the Jesus movement in Kansas City. And the International Charismatic Conference of 1977 gathered fifty-thousand believers into Arrowhead Stadium from all denominations to proclaim Christian unity to a world riddled by the Vietnam War and social revolutions, a world hungry for peace.

When the citizens of a hundred years ago dubbed our city "the prophetic city," they had no idea how fitting the name would become. What started as "fifteen square miles at the mouth of the Kaw" has today grown to a city of 319 square miles—a land whose development began with the work and inspiration of missionaries, prophets, evangelists, and preachers. This is their story. This is our story.

Next to Deatherage's history, you will find another book written the same year. Historian Olive Hoggins wrote a one hundred year history of the churches in Kansas City: *The Centenary History of Kansas City Churches*. In her introduction, she writes, "This work endeavors to show how the spirit of religion, inherent in our forefathers, is woven into the very warp and woof of the life of this marvelously grown city." To illustrate the church's centrality, she gives the history of every church that had been founded in Kansas City from the time the first French fur traders settled in 1820 until her time in 1927—all 367 churches. Amazingly, after Hoggins's history, no historian wrote a book on church history for the next hundred years. It is high time another book on "the prophetic city" records what God has done.

In her book, Hoggins tells the story of every single church. Eighty years after her book, the 2010 US Census reported 2,271 religious places of worship (Christian or other) in the metro area. It would be impossible, although amazing, to tell the story of each one. Inevitably as you read the book, you will think, "They left out the story of . . ." You're right. We left out countless stories that never made the history books.

Instead, this book is a highlights reel. It's a collection of some of the essential stories that allow us to understand the spiritual roots of our city in a deeper way. Marcus Garvey said it this way: "A people without the knowledge of their past history, origin and culture is like a tree without roots." But our purpose is simple. As we gain an understanding of where the church has been, perhaps we can better understand where we ought to go in the future.

DISCOVERING THE PAST TO SHAPE OUR FUTURE

How to Read This Book
...

You'll find a few resources included at the back of this book that can be used for more in-depth study. We hope these items encourage you to further explore God's work in Kansas City:

"God's Plan for Cities"—Based off pastor Tim Keller's "Theology of Cities" as well as local Christian leaders' insights, this article provides a summary of the general purpose of cities: why God created them and the role they play in both society and in God's kingdom. In many regards, Kansas City has a unique history, but it also shares elements typical of every city. Cities protect the vulnerable, foster creativity, and reveal God. The article also addresses how we respond to cities. Do cities determine our lives, or do we determine the life of the city? And how does God's sovereignty fit into this equation? Come with us as we examine God's role in the life of a city.

Discussion Questions—History goes beyond mere stories of the past. History helps us to both interpret the present and to predict the future. As you read how, time after time, a few people revolutionized an entire city, we hope these stories become inspiration and blueprints for what you can do. To facilitate the connection between the past and the present, we have included study guide questions. The questions will help you discover the wisdom history offers for navigating current issues facing the church. The questions include Scripture references to help shape your interpretation of history, as well as a list of other relevant Scriptures, if your group would like a more in-depth Bible study.

We hope the discussion questions encourage you to process this book as a community. In writing the book, we were struck by the fact that every historic movement in Kansas City happened in a group. Believers connected with other like-minded people and effected change. We hope the study questions encourage your Bible study or small group to brainstorm together to find out what role God would have you play in the next chapter of our city's history.

Timeline—Although the events in each chapter are written in chronological order, for the sake of the overall story, we separated historic events into chapters based on themes. This means that some simultaneous events are separated into different chapters.

We hope the timeline helps you piece together the overlap of different events and serves as a quick reference for Kansas City's church history. We also added a few events to the timeline that were not included in the book's main text, but which we felt were worth mentioning in the overall summary of our history.

Bibliography—We did the research, so you don't have to! But for those who are curious, we have included a bibliography of sources for further study. It lists books, news articles, online resources, and the names of community members whom we interviewed for the book. The list is by no means exhaustive of Kansas City's historic resources. The items are simply the sources we drew from when writing this book.

Tours—Beyond the resources in the back of the book, you can further engage the history of Kansas City through a guided tour with The Signatry. As you travel to key historic spots, listen to the little-known stories of the Christians who formed our city. Discover the real McCoy in Westport, view the river as Lewis and Clark first saw it, stand on the stones of the Liberty Memorial and hear about the Christian philanthropist who led its construction, and more. Visit thesignatry.com/KCRoots to request a tour.

What Is "Church"?

Throughout this book, we will often use the word "church" to designate a specific group of believers who gather regularly for worship, often in a building (e.g. First Baptist Church of Kansas City). However, we recognize that in the Bible, the word "church" generally refers to a broader group of people: all who believe in the death and resurrection of Jesus as the payment for sin and the promise of eternal life. The Bible does not separate these believers into different churches or denominations. Their only separation is based on geography. As you read stories of Kansas City's different churches, remember that Jesus sees us as one church—the church in Kansas City.

    Second, remember that Jesus adores His church. We are His prized possession. He is head over heels in love with us. In Ephesians 5:25-27, Paul elevates Christ's affection for His church as the pinnacle of true love. He writes, "Husbands, love your wives as Christ loved the church and gave himself up for her to make her holy, cleansing her by the washing with water through the Word, and to present her to himself as a radiant church, without stain or wrinkle or any other blemish, but holy and blameless" (NIV). The church is Jesus's favorite, and He gave His life for her. As you read the pages ahead, you'll find beautiful stories of believers' victories. However, you'll also read stories of failure, confusion, and brokenness. Remember that despite our mess, Jesus still adores His church. He gave His blood for every mistake, and He glows with pride over every success. We are His bride.

Chapter 1
Fur Traders and Missionaries
...
(1804 - 1850)

Today, you can travel to the mouth of the Kaw River, or Kansas River, to see the roots of our city. There, you feel the ground itself shake as trains roar by the shipping yards of the West Bottoms. Semis thunder overhead on I-70, which spans the Missouri River.

Looking across the sparkling river, you see the skyline of Kansas City—silver-blue skyscrapers clustered together in a patch, popping out of the thick foliage of trees covering the riverbank. You hear the click of giant crane booms as they put up new apartments and hotels in the heart of the city. A white plane descends toward the runway of the downtown airport.

At Kaw Point, the Kansas River unites with the Missouri River and flows as one. Kaw Point is the spot where Lewis and Clark landed during their expedition. It is now a tourist spot—with rocky landscaping, a walking trail, and markers for a bike path. You can find the starting point for the path in the River Market downtown. At the river's edge, you can still see the caked dirt where the water level has receded, where the muddy riverbank has hardened in the sunlight, cracking into haphazard lines of dried mud—the same shoreline the first explorers would have landed on.

Walking along the riverbank, you can't help but imagine this landscape before civilization encroached—before the noise of airports, highways, and railroads—when all that could be heard were the soft dips of canoe paddles as explorers pushed upriver. They would have passed a small, brown turtle basking in the sunlight—a turtle that slipped from the rock into the water as it heard their canoe oars coming closer. They would see the turtle's back slowly drifting along the water, waiting for the intruders to pass.

Lewis and Clark

On June 26, 1804, Meriwether Lewis and William Clark slowly paddled up the Missouri River. They met no residents. Unknown to them, the Kanza tribe who lived in the area was away on a buffalo hunt. There were no states of Kansas or Missouri—only the Kanza, Osage, and Otoe-Missouria tribes that thrived there, living off the land's abundant natural resources.

Clark recorded in his journal that the party landed their boats at the southern shore of the Missouri River and set up camp for three days by the mouth of the Kansas River. They set out over the wooded hills and bluffs hunting deer. They repaired canoes and regrouped for the journey ahead. The humidity hung thick as Clark pulled out a journal damp with the morning's dew, leafed to the next

The Lewis and Clark Monument in Quality Hill commemorates their party's first landing in Kansas City in 1804.

blank page and recorded, "The country about the mouth of this river is very fine, as well as the north of the Missouri." He also explored the area just south of the Missouri River, climbing the place that is now Quality Hill, where the Lewis and Clark Monument stands today.

> *"The river has always brought both the good and bad to our city."*

(Present-day Quality Hill is a historic neighborhood situated on a two-hundred foot high bluff overlooking the West Bottoms.) Clark wrote, "The highlands comes to the river Kansas on the upper side at about a mile, full in view, and a beautiful place for a fort, good landing place," although he added a note after tasting the river that "the waters of the Kansas is very disagreeably tasted to me."

Apparently others in their party did not care for the water either. The last day of their stay at Kaw Point, Clark's travel journal turns into makeshift court records. One of their crew members, John Collins, talked Hugh Hall into sneaking him some whiskey while Hall was supposed to be guarding it. Collins then proceeded to get drunk while on duty. Clark's journal records the makeshift trial they held at the riverbank after the crew discovered the crime. They were alone in the wilderness, yet they held Collins and Hall as prisoners. One member of Lewis and Clark's party acted as judge; four others, as court members. The makeshift court sentenced Collins to one hundred lashes for getting drunk while on his post and sentenced Hall to fifty lashes for sneaking Collins the whiskey "contrary to all order, rule, or regulation."

This story is more than an entertaining morsel from the first annals of Kansas City history. The trial exposes the raw humanity of those who went before us, even in our earliest days. In reading history, we can easily romanticize historic figures as perfect people who accomplished great feats. But this story exposes they were people just like us—one man got drunk, the others decided to whip him as punishment, then they continued their journey. As you read history, keep reality in mind. The river has always brought both the good and the bad to our city.

After Collins' and Hall's trial and punishment, Lewis records that the party then set out from the Kansas River at about four-thirty that afternoon. They continued paddling up the Missouri River, forging the way for all who would follow in their ripple.

The First Settlers

The first permanent European settlers arrived over fifteen years later in 1821. Francois Chouteau became the first French settler to make his home at the spot where the Kansas and Missouri Rivers met. As a twenty-four-year-old newlywed, he traveled with his bride, Berenice, upriver from St. Louis to stake out a trading post.

Francois came from a line of starters. His grandfather, Pierre Laclede Liguest, helped found the city of St. Louis. Francois grew up in St. Louis, and he likely met Lewis and Clark as a child when they stayed at his home, hosted by his father, Jean Pierre Chouteau. Francois's family had a monopoly trading fur with the Osage tribe that lived along the Missouri River. His father belonged to the ranks of the wealthy, prominent men in St. Louis. Jean Pierre Chouteau hosted the Lewis and Clark expedition when they launched from St. Louis, and the explorers even invited him later to Washington, D.C., to celebrate the return of their voyage. He accepted their invitation and went to Washington even though he spoke no English, only French.

Coming from an elite and experienced family perfectly equipped Francois to start a new city. It boiled in his blood. Also in his blood ran a strong faith in Jesus. Both he and Berenice came from Catholic families. Together, they brought their faith with them to this new settlement at the mouth of the Kaw.

The Chouteaus settled at the mouth of the Kaw (Kansas) River, the spot Lewis and Clark might have raved about to him and his father on their return. He stopped at a small landing and set up a trading post. This spot is roughly where present-day Troost Road would intersect with the river if the road continued straight north. Chouteau built a small warehouse along the edge of the river. In the warehouse, Chouteau kept the goods to be traded with the Native Americans—blankets, pots, guns, tools, and cloth. He would take these goods, paddle up the Kansas River to where the Kanza Indians lived, and trade with them.

The Kanza (also "Kaw" or "Kansa") were known as proud warriors who lived in what is present-day northern and eastern Kansas. Their hunting grounds stretched throughout the western plains, and they frequently migrated in this area hunting buffalo. Explorers described the warriors as "erect, dignified and proud; sometimes even scornful," according to historian William E. Unrau's book *The Kansa Indians*. Explorers also told stories of the Kanza women's strength—they could carry one-hundred-pound loads for miles or deliver a baby in the morning and still go about their chores that same evening.

The young Kanza men were raised to be strong-spirited and independent. At age twelve or thirteen, as a rite of passage, each boy was sent on a "vision quest"—four days alone without food or water. Unrau records, "During this time he was to invoke the spirits by introspection, wailing, and in some cases self-infliction of bodily torture." Dreams, visions, and "supernatural phenomena" that occurred were supposed to be a preview of the boy's future.

Because they lived off the buffalo herds that roamed the plains, the Kanza were adept hunters. When they found out the French would pay dearly for animal fur, they began trapping beaver, otter, deer, muskrat, and raccoon. They would then trade the furs to Chouteau's men in exchange for the goods they wanted.

Chouteau would take the furs and store them in his warehouse. Then come springtime, as the ice chunks thawed and disappeared from the Missouri River, Chouteau would load the furs on the flatbed keelboat and ship them downriver. He founded the Berthold, Chouteau, and Pratte Company, which became the western division of the American Fur Company owned by the famous John Jacob Astor out east. Fur trading brought in a good income, and over time a couple hundred French fur traders moved to Chouteau's trading post.

More and more French moved to the area, and they took Kanza women as their wives. As early as 1802, fur trader Perrin Du Lac records of his interaction with a Kanza village: "They feasted me by turns, and, according to their customs, offered me their daughters. I accepted those of the great chief, whom I was afraid of displeasing by a refusal." Du Lac noted that "to accept" a daughter of a chief was necessary in order to conduct trade.

The children of the French and the Kanzas were known as the metis, or "in-betweens," since they were both French and Kanzan. Into this community, traveling Catholic priests came to minister. Beginning in 1826, Father Joseph Lutz and Father Benedict Roux took turns traveling to the area to preach. Father Lutz spoke out against his fellow Frenchmen. "They are slothful bellies," said Lutz, "and not much different from the Cretans, addicted to drink and much talking, ignorant to pass over in silence the rest of their vices. . . . Some of them live with Indian concubines, refusing the grace offered to them by my ministry. Only two could I prevail upon to dismiss their concubines and contract in legitimate marriages."

When Francois settled Chouteau's trading post, he had missionary priests come and minister to his family and the men at his warehouse.

The First Church

By the early 1830s, at least a hundred French settlers had made their home in the community. The settlement thrived, except for one problem: It lacked a church. In the neighboring town of Independence, St. Mary's Parish had been founded in 1823, but no formal place of worship had been built at Chouteau's trading post.

The Chouteaus were wealthy. Francois Chouteau's brother had joined them by this point, and the families wanted a church. The traveling priests would come and go, but the Chouteaus wanted a church for their enclave. They asked one of the priests, Father Benedict Roux, to build a church.

It is worth noting that the first church was made possible by a gift: The Chouteaus and their extended family donated significantly for the church to be built. Once the church was erected, the community officially named the small log cabin parish St. Regis Francis, but everyone around the area referred to it as "Chouteau's Church," since many of its parishioners were family members or employees of the Chouteaus.

They built the church, but with it came a small tiff. This community was known for their balls, dances they would host. The air filled with fiddle music and laughter as they danced around the fire and feasted on corn bread and hearty bouillon soup. Father Roux ministered to the parish as priest at the time. He had been assigned to this burgeoning congregation. Roux came as an outsider to the metis, to the French fur traders, and to this new community. He came and preached against the dances they held. The only problem? Berenice Chouteau, the leading lady of the city, threw the dances.

"They are harmless," she insisted to Father Roux. She continued to hold the dances, and he continued to preach against them.

Roux wrote back to the bishop complaining they didn't listen to him and complaining of Berenice, "She leads all the French people here by the nose." Still, Roux built up a little congregation. Despite his complaints that the people didn't listen to him, he baptized forty-eight people in just one year. Somewhere he found followers.

As American settlers started immigrating to the area, Roux found them to be a more responsive audience than the French. He began holding bilingual services, preaching both in French and in his rough English. At this point, Missouri had just become a state, but unclaimed hills and woods still dominated its landscape. Before becoming a state, the land had been part of the Louisiana territory

The "Chouteau's Church" historic marker stands at the spot of the city's first church, a small log-cabin parish, where they later built the Cathedral of the Immaculate Conception.

> "She leads all the French people here by the nose."
>
> -Fr. Roux

belonging to the French, explaining why many French people still lived in the area.

Roux wrote back to his bishop about his American parishioners, "They listen with the greatest patience to my poor English."

Looking back on the mark Father Roux and the Chouteaus left on Kansas City, you'll see the petty differences fade into the background. They argued about the dances, but they also began a legacy of faith for an entire city. Their first goal was to build a church for their community, no matter the cost.

Then and Now

Have you ever heard of Johnson County? If so, perhaps you've been to Shawnee Mission Park or driven Shawnee Mission Parkway. Johnson County is named after the missionary Reverend Thomas Johnson who started a mission to the Shawnee tribe.

Missionaries Follow

President Andrew Jackson urged Congress to pass the Indian Removal Act of 1830. The Indian Removal Act ordered the displacement of thousands of Native Americans from the East Coast, banishing them to the western plains. Three tribes—the Shawnee, the Delaware, and the Wyandot (Does Wyandotte County sound familiar?)—eventually relocated to the area that is now Kansas City, where the Kansas River and Missouri River join. At that time, no Kansas City existed—only bluffs, woods, and rivers.

The Shawnee tribe originally lived in the eastern region of the United States and had maintained a rich cultural heritage for hundreds of years. They hunted, fished, and farmed. Elk was their most important game animal. They made pottery and carvings. They believed in a Great Spirit as the supreme power. He rewarded those who pleased him and punished those who displeased him. The Shawnee believed the Great Spirit created a woman, and she created the rest of the world. Every year they held a bread dance and offered loaves to the Shawnee deity.

However, as Europeans encroached, they pushed the Shawnee out of their lands, and the Shawnee scattered to different locations. Some ended up in eastern Missouri, and in 1826 they relocated to

CHAPTER 1

KANSAS CITY LEGACY
• • •
Father Bernard Donnelly

"THE RIGHTEOUS WILL BE REMEMBERED FOREVER..." PSALM 112:6

Another Catholic priest, Father Bernard Donnelly, came to Kansas City in 1845, and he served the community for the next thirty-five years, working to build up both the spiritual and civic strength of the community. Donnelly introduced formal education to the area. He taught classes in an unfinished basement of the Cathedral of the Immaculate Conception before it was completed. He also served the children of the community by opening an asylum for orphans.

A historical marker at the Cathedral of the Immaculate Conception (the site of Kansas City's first church) commemorates him as "a friend to all, regardless of creed or color." In 1880 *The Kansas City Journal* said of Donnelly, "One of the most marked traits of this good man was his benevolence and charity, the crowning glory of which was the Asylum for Orphans . . . As long as Kansas City exists, his name will be one of her household treasures and be cherished as that of her pioneer priest."

Donnelly Avenue commemorates Father Bernard Donnelly, one of the first priests to serve Kansas City.

the Kansas River area. In 1832, after the Indian Removal Act, another group of Shawnee was forced to relocate from Ohio to Kansas. Historian James H. Howard tells of their journey. "Great hardships were endured by the Shawnees on the trip west," he writes. "Whiskey traders, government bungling of supply deliveries, and illness augmented the difficulties."

As the Shawnee trickled into the region, missionaries followed. In July 1830, Chief Fish of the Shawnee tribe wrote to the Methodist Mission Board requesting that they send a missionary teacher to open a school for the tribe.

In response to the chief's request, the Methodist Mission Board sent Reverend Thomas Johnson to the Shawnee tribe. The year he came to the Shawnee, Johnson had just married his wife Sarah Davis. The two of them moved from Missouri to what is now Wyandotte County to open a school for the Shawnee. Johnson built a school where children of different tribes boarded to learn basic academics, manual arts, and agriculture. And of course, he also included evangelism as part of his ministry.

After living in the area for just a few years, Johnson wrote in a letter to a fellow minister, "We have great excitement in the Indian country; some of the leading men of the Shawnee nation have lately surrendered their prejudices; twelve or fourteen have lately joined our society. The Peoria nation has submitted to the yoke of Christ; forty of them joined last Sabbath week."

Over the years, the mission continued to grow, and the school turned into an entire outpost—hence the name Shawnee Mission. At the height of its operations, it had sixteen buildings and over two hundred acres of land. It served not only the Shawnee, but over a dozen other tribes in the area. Today, only three of

Johnson County's namesake, Reverend Thomas Johnson, began a missionary school for the displaced Shawnee after the Indian Removal Act. His mission buildings still stand today in Fairway, Kansas.

COURTESY OF KANSAS STATE HISTORICAL SOCIETY

the buildings remain standing at the Shawnee Indian Mission State Historic Site in Fairway, Kansas.

While Johnson ministered to the Shawnee tribe, other missionaries came to the area as well. After the Indian Removal Act, many missionaries moved westward to minister to the newly-arrived Native Americans, hoping to convert them to Christianity and to the ways of white people. Some tribes resented white encroachment, while other tribes valued these missionaries as mediators between their peoples, the US government, and other settlers. As Native Americans saw their land disappearing and their old way of life becoming impossible to maintain, they asked for missionaries to come and help them adapt to the changes.

Reverend Isaac McCoy came to the area as a missionary to the displaced Native Americans. He was a strong Baptist and missionary at heart. He felt for the Native Americans and wanted to minister to them. He established formal mission outposts in Indiana and Michigan. But his evangelistic efforts reached into Kansas, Oklahoma, and Nebraska. In 1811, his son John Calvin McCoy was born. The reverend named his son after the theologian John Calvin, indicating the family's deep Christian faith. Later, John Calvin McCoy would become known as the Father of Kansas City.

McCoy and his family traveled west up the Missouri River. Along with them, McCoy's son-in-law Dr. Johnston Lykins traveled with them. (Lykins would later become the second mayor of Kansas City, Missouri.) They started a series of Baptist missions throughout the new Native American territory where the Kansas River met the Missouri River.

McCoy's first taste of life on the reservation came with the culture shock typical of most missionaries. He stayed in a Kanza village in 1828. The Kanza families shared huts and cooked indoors, with a hole in the ceiling for the smoke to escape.

Reverend Isaac McCoy came to Kansas City as a Baptist missionary to serve the Native American tribes. His son became known as the Father of Kansas City.

COURTESY OF KANSAS STATE HISTORICAL SOCIETY

DISCOVERING THE PAST TO SHAPE OUR FUTURE

Unrau summarizes McCoy's report: "Half the village appeared to crowd into the lodge assigned to him; children cried without interruption, adults screamed wildly, and the air was so saturated with smoke from the fireplaces and tobacco pipes that he was forced to punch a hole in the wall in order to breathe."

However, as he grew to understand their culture, he began to love them. McCoy and Lykins did things differently than other missionaries of the time. Instead of trying to conform the Native Americans to the white men's language and customs, they learned the tribes' native languages and translated hymns into their languages. McCoy and Lykins wanted to engage them in a way that would be meaningful and understandable. Historian Bertha Ellen Milstead wrote concerning the Baptist missionaries under McCoy's supervision, "These missionaries by learning the language and by publishing school books, songs, and parts of the gospels in the native languages had been able to reach the people in a wider and deeper way than those who were unable to [learn the language]."

Their strategies were very effective. A bystander wrote of their meetings, "[O]n many occasions the power of God was so strong in the meetings the Indians would begin shouting with joy, other times the translators and preachers had to stop because the power of God was so strong. The glory of those meetings spread to many of the Indians and many were saved."

McCoy loved his work as a missionary. He wrote,

> "The power of God was so strong in the meetings, the Indians would begin shouting with joy . . ."

I would rather be a missionary to the Indians than fill the President's chair or sit on the throne of Alexander, emperor of Russia. I would rather preach Jesus to the poor Indians in a bark camp than address the thousands who assemble in Samson Street meeting house, Philadelphia. Something has turned my attention towards the Indians, and every feeling of my soul is enlisted in their cause, yet still I may be wrong. But I feel not the least inclination to turn back but would drive on with the vehemence of Peter, the meekness of Moses and the wisdom of Solomon.

McCoy worked tirelessly for the rights of the Native American tribes who had been displaced. He drafted a colonization plan for them that set aside territory where they could live without fear of the white people encroaching on their land. He wrote, "The day for cold speculations, and tedious theories, respecting the fate of the aborigines of America, has gone by. . . . Are we what we profess to be—THE FRIENDS OF THE INDIANS? Then let us manifest our faith by our works." He proposed his plan to the US Congress. It was received, approved, and signed by the president. Over his lifetime, McCoy made nine trips to Washington, D.C., a month-long trek during the pioneer days, and advocated on behalf of the Native American tribes, asking that the US government create a sovereign territory for them.

A Foundation for the City

From its very founding, Kansas City has been missional. Catholic fur traders built the first church at what is now the heart of downtown Kansas City. A Baptist missionary and his entrepreneurial son founded Westport, the seedling of Kansas City. A Methodist missionary, Reverend Johnson, started a mission to the Shawnee Indians, beginning what are now Wyandotte County and Johnson County. Through and through, Kansas City has Christian roots. As historian Olive Hoggins stated, our founders' deep faith "is woven into the very warp and woof" of our city.

While we recognize our missional foundations, we don't romanticize the past. The river brought both the good and bad. The Chouteaus started the first church, but other Frenchmen accepted Kanza women as their concubines and refused to listen to the priest who spoke out against this practice. Berenice Chouteau and Father Roux never agreed on the dances.

And yet, despite these problems, the church persisted. Mrs. Chouteau and Father Roux never saw eye to eye, yet they moved beyond their differences, working together for the common goal of building a church. McCoy and Johnson pushed beyond pioneer struggles and cultural differences to serve Native Americans. Filled with compassion and a vision for how their ministry could make a difference, these pioneers forged a path and, in doing so, laid a foundation for Christianity in the city.

Chapter 2
A Faulty Auction and a Flood

...

(1838 - 1860)

Isaac McCoy's son, John Calvin McCoy, grew up seeing firsthand his father's dedication and the power of God in the missionary meetings. His entire life, he carried the same faith as his father. In 1889, at John Calvin McCoy's funeral, Dr. Nathan Scarritt, a Methodist minister, said, "Christ's atonement was the rock on which his faith was founded."

John Calvin McCoy carried the same strong Christian faith as his father, but he was not a minister. He was an entrepreneur. A builder. A strategist. His father built churches and missions, but in 1833 John Calvin established Westport as a trading post. At that time in our nation's history, Westport was the proverbial convenience store. The pioneers launched from Independence. They traveled west from St. Louis on the Missouri River (the highway of the time) up to the small town of Independence. From there, they gathered supplies and prepared for the several month long trek to Santa Fe, California, or Oregon.

Just twelve miles outside of Independence, they came across Westport, McCoy's small trading post. Like a convenience store, here they might stock up on any last-minute items they'd forgotten in Independence. There they could receive friendly conversation, words of caution about the trail's conditions, and perhaps a kind-hearted blessing for the journey. But McCoy's post would be their last taste of civilization for months.

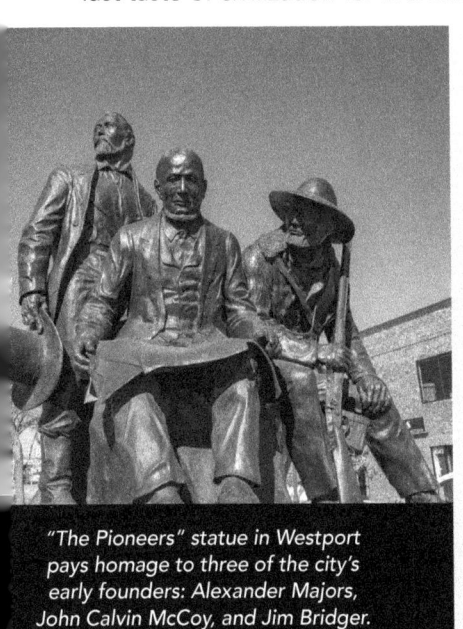

"The Pioneers" statue in Westport pays homage to three of the city's early founders: Alexander Majors, John Calvin McCoy, and Jim Bridger.

Then and Now

Perhaps you've driven down Broadway to where it intersects with Westport Road, just four miles south of the river. You'll notice there's an odd little traffic loop—it's not a parking lot; it's not a road—it's just a weird loop in front of small local businesses like the Corner Restaurant and Computers to Go. In the middle of the loop stands a statue of three men: John Calvin McCoy in the center, with two men on either side of him (Alexander Majors and Jim Bridger). This loop is where traders used to circle their wagons when they dropped off goods at Westport. They would land on the river, drive the four miles down Broadway to Westport, get their supplies, drop off other traded goods, and head back to the river. And still today, we have this little loop as an obnoxious traffic pattern where it's hard to park, too narrow to turn around, with no stoplights or stop signs to direct a way out. But it's still there two hundred years later, thanks to John Calvin McCoy.

A Fraudulent Auction

By the mid 1830s, the area consisted primarily of two separate settlements—Chouteau's Trading Post and Westport. How did these two settlements eventually become Kansas City? It took an entrepreneur, a tragic death, and a fraudulent auction.

McCoy was an entrepreneur. To obtain supplies for his trading post, he had to trek four miles from Westport down to the river. The trail upon which he drove would have taken him down what is now Broadway Boulevard. He would have passed Chouteau's Church at Twelfth Street. The area probably contained a total of five hundred settlers.

The spot where the riverboats landed for McCoy's supplies was owned by a wealthy Frenchman, Gabriel Prudhomme. He owned 257 acres of land on the south edge of the Missouri River—between what are now Broadway Boulevard and Troost Avenue, as far south as Independence Avenue. Tragically, Prudhomme was killed in a brawl, leaving behind his pregnant wife, six children, and his land. His wife was unable to maintain the land, and it had to be put up for auction.

Enter another character in the story: James McGee. (You've likely heard of McGee Street in downtown Kansas City.) McGee was wealthy, and the community knew him as being land-hungry. He had already bought up multiple properties around the area, and he now set his eye on the Prudhomme property. McGee was named trustee of the estate, and after years in limbo the courts ordered that the property be sold at auction.

On July 7, 1838, McGee held an auction for the highest bidder. McGee, supposedly to save the estate money, declared himself auctioneer. McCoy and the other future city leaders attended the auction and planned to make a bid for the property. However, McGee started the auction and opened the bidding at $1,800. Some accounts claim that before anyone could bid, the property was declared sold to Abraham Fonda. Even in those days, the price of $1,800 was an unusually low price for prime riverfront landing property.

McCoy and the others suspected collusion. Sure enough, it came out that Abraham Fonda, a stranger in town, had conspired with McGee to purchase the land cheaply at the auction so that he could later sell it to McGee. McCoy and the other leaders cried foul and sued McGee. The trial ended with McGee being convicted as guilty.

Four months after the auction, the judge voided the auction and held another auction for the land, this time with the county sheriff in charge instead of McGee. This second time around, McCoy and twelve other men formed the Town Company of Kansas. They pooled their money and took out loans to be able to purchase the land. They formed a plan to create a town at the edge of the river, just four miles north of Westport. Their bid was the winning bid.

They debated names for the new town, rejecting suggestions such as Port Fonda, Rabbitville, and Possum Trot, and finally settling on the Town of Kansas—which would ultimately become Kansas City.

A Flood Establishes Kansas City

The beginning of the Town of Kansas was rocky. Colonel William Chick became the first postmaster, and he built a warehouse as well. But other lot sales were slow. McCoy and the other members of the Kansas Town Company tried to sell properties to developers, but they couldn't. Disagreements, lawsuits, financial difficulties, deaths, and a holdup in the transfer of the deed and title to the property all served to stall the sale of land. As sales lagged, the Kansas Town Company struggled to pay off the loans it had taken in buying the land.

At the time the Town of Kansas was formed, Independence was the dominant landing for riverboats. Independence was where the wagon trains began their trail drives. Independence was the key point of commerce. Independence was the major launching point for the Santa Fe Trail, the Oregon Trail, and the California Trail.

Then the river saved the day.

In 1844, heavy rains caused the Missouri River to overflow its banks. The Kansas River spilled into the Missouri River, flooding the West Bottoms and the Missouri's main channel. The flood wiped out Chouteau's trading post. Berenice Chouteau's warehouse and farm disappeared, as well as small stores, a ferry, and a storage building in the Town of Kansas. Chouteau's Church, however, survived. The only business that survived was William M. Chick's warehouse, thanks to a dramatic rescue by John Calvin McCoy. *Kansas City: An American Story* records the rescue:

> A surprised Chick fled with his family to a nearby hill, while his daughter, a Mrs. Peery, plunged through the water on horseback. She rode to McCoy's house and summoned his help. McCoy went immediately to the ferry, rounded up 20 men and undertook to run the boat to Chick's house to save his belongings. The rescuers found the water almost to the second floor, so they tore off part of Chick's roof and took out what furniture they could. . . . All other property and houses in the bottoms were swept away.

As disastrous as the flood was, it proved providential. What seemed to destroy the little Town of Kansas—a flood that wiped out much of the town just struggling to survive—actually created its destiny.

The flood changed the course of the river and uncovered a rock landing. Calvin McCoy recognized the new rock ledge as a potential landing for riverboats—a perfect spot for the pioneers and traders to land, unload their trade, and embark on the pioneer trail.

> **"What seemed to destroy the little Town of Kansas . . . actually created its destiny."**

Before the flood, Independence claimed fame as the major launching point for the Santa Fe trail, the Oregon trail, and the California trail. But after the flood rerouted the river, McCoy reasoned that since the river offered smooth traveling, it made more sense for travelers to go upriver past Independence to the Town of Kansas, then get off, go to Westport, get their goods, and set off on the trail westward. Using the new landing would save pioneers eighteen miles of land travel, allowing them to avoid crossing the treacherous Blue River by Independence. Once the flood changed the river landing, the property of the Town of Kansas became much more desirable and valuable, and people started buying it up.

KANSAS CITY LEGACY
...
Berenice Chouteau

"THE RIGHTEOUS WILL BE REMEMBERED FOREVER..." PSALM 112:6

Berenice Chouteau came to be known as the "Grand Dame" of Kansas City. She was devoted and dedicated to the people there, even after her husband, Francois, passed away. The Chouteaus always had excellent relations with the Native Americans, and when a cholera outbreak occurred in 1854, Berenice rode on horseback to the neighboring Native American villages to care for their sick. A Chouteau Society historical marker records that she provided burial shrouds for those who died from the epidemic, and when she ran out of cloth, she even used the fabric from her own wedding dress to cover those who had passed away. The society states, "She outlived her nine children and died in 1888 at the age of eighty-seven, having gained the love and respect of all Kansas Citians."

God, in His sovereignty, used the Missouri River to make us Kansas City. If not for the flood, we would have been the Independence metropolitan area. But because of the flood and because of McCoy's foresight to build up the city, we have Kansas City as it is today.

The Rise of the Church and Three Church Builders

Colonel Chick, in addition to being a postmaster, was also a religious man. He offered his home in 1840 as a place to hold a worship service for a pioneer Methodist preacher, Rev. James Porter. After the flood, in 1845, they gathered again in Chick's yard. Dr. Nathan Scarritt wrote about that day, "The weather being warm, and the congregation large, the service was held near the house in the open air under the shade of some forest trees. After preaching, the preacher [Porter] requested those who wished to join the church to take their seats on a log near where he stood. Five came forward and took their seats accordingly." Those five people and Porter became the first Methodist church, as well as the first official Protestant church in Kansas City.

While the fledgling towns of Kansas and Westport were in their infancy, several key men rose up alongside the McCoys and shaped the Protestant church in Kansas City. Historian Olive Hoggins lists Thomas M. James, Dr. Nathan Scarritt, and John B. Wornall as "Kansas City's three great church builders." James's son wrote of the three church builders, "The two men most like [my father] in the building of the churches in Kansas City were the Rev. Nathan Scarritt of the Methodist Church and John B. Wornall of the Westport Baptist Church. To these three men, master builders and always fast friends, is due much of the religious growth of the Protestant churches of this city."

In 1855, James and his wife Sarah joined Dr. Johnston Lykins (Isaac McCoy's missionary sidekick) and seven other people in founding First Baptist Church of Kansas City, including Robert and Mary Ann Holmes. (Does "Holmes Road" sound familiar?) The church was the second Protestant church in Kansas City, after the Methodist church. According to Hoggins, over his lifetime James

"There's gold in them hills!"

You've most likely heard of the California gold rush where prospectors flocked to California after hearing gold was found at John Sutter's mill. But the gold rush would have never happened without the generosity of John Calvin McCoy.

McCoy's daughter Nellie told the story of a man who ventured through Westport while she was a little girl. The man's business venture had failed, and he went to McCoy desperate and suicidal. McCoy reasoned with him and convinced him not to give up. Nellie writes, "My father offered to lend him money to pay off his indebtedness, though his own purse was a slender one; at the same time offering to help him to continue his proposed journey onward." McCoy and some other merchants equipped the man and his assistant with horses and provisions for the journey. The man was John Sutter. He continued to California, where he built a sawmill. A few years later, he struck gold.

Because of the gold rush, over the following years, forty thousand gold miners passed through Westport and the Town of Kansas (now Kansas City). Their spending, and the growing Santa Fe and Oregon trades, plus increasing local commerce, netted the merchants of the area over $5 million in 1850. McCoy's generosity of a horse and a few supplies paid off far beyond what he could have dreamed.

contributed significantly to the number of churches in Kansas City, giving "personal supervision to the construction of three Baptist church buildings." Considering that by 1857, the city boasted only seven churches total, adding three churches would have been an impressive feat.

The Scarritt Renaissance neighborhood exemplifies Scarritt's influence throughout Kansas City.

The Scarritt Point historical marker stands at the northeast corner of the Kansas City Museum.

Then and Now

Readers might recognize the name "Scarritt" from Scarritt Elementary that operated until 2016, from the Scarritt Renaissance neighborhood in Northeast Kansas City, or perhaps from the historical marker on the northwest corner of the Kansas City Museum. The "Scarritt Point" marker stands as a solitary stone plaque overlooking Cliff Drive and the rolling bluffs of George E. Kessler Park in Northeast Kansas City.

Scarritt balanced dual roles as both a pastor and an investor. In the mid-1800s, ministers commonly traveled between congregations since the sparsely populated pioneer communities could not support a full-time minister. Scarritt pastored five Methodist churches in Kansas City and traveled among the Native American reservations to preach. Always missional at heart, he longed to see Kansas City become a launching pad for missionaries. He established a Bible school and a training school for missionaries.

In addition to pastoring, Scarritt invested in real estate. He earned a fortune of $2 million from buying and selling farmland. Although he became a multimillionaire, he never lost sight of true wealth. He valued his faith more than any prestige that money

CHAPTER 2

> "The title of Sonship to Himself . . . I esteem as infinitely more precious than any title with which mortal man could honor me."
>
> -Dr. Nathan Scarritt

Dr. Nathan Scarritt served both the Methodist Churches in Kansas City and the Native American reservations nearby.

could offer, writing, "The titles of Sonship to Himself, which I believe God by his Spirit has written upon my inmost heart, I esteem as infinitely more precious than any title with which mortal man could honor me."

Then and Now

Most Kansas City residents associate the name "Wornall" with the road stretching from the Country Club Plaza to the southern tip of Kansas City at 135th Street. They may have also attended a wedding or event at the John Wornall House Museum located off Wornall Road in Brookside. Both the road and the museum were named after John B. Wornall, one of the three church planters of Kansas City.

Scarritt treasured his close friendship with the third church builder, John B. Wornall. Wornall suffered several personal tragedies throughout his life: Both his mother and brother died in the same year. In the years that followed, he lost two wives and six out of ten children. Despite facing numerous tragedies, Wornall remained active in his faith and community. In 1845, two years after moving to Westport, Wornall joined Westport Baptist Church. He became an active member of the congregation, serving as treasurer and moderator. Though a dedicated church member, his civic involvement

THE SPIRITUAL ROOTS OF KANSAS CITY

extended far beyond his church. He served as chairman of William Jewell College's board of trustees, co-founded Kansas City National Bank in 1870, and even served four years on the Missouri State Senate.

Wornall's legacy of church service continued after his death in 1892. In 1916, his third wife, Roma Wornall, helped raise money to buy the property where Wornall Road Baptist Church still stands. His son John Wornall loaned the money for the church building's construction.

The River Brings Diversity

The Town of Kansas began as a river town. From the city's earliest start, the river brought diversity to the area in the form of new cultures

John B. Wornall, one of Kansas City's "three great church builders," joined the Westport Baptist Church in 1845.

and worldviews. Before there were interstates, and even before railroads, there were rivers. America's river systems served as the nation's highways. *Kansas City: An American Story* says, "Rivers were the superhighways of the American frontier, and boats were the over-the-road trucks." The rivers connected civilizations, and this was especially true of the Missouri River. As the farthest river branch leading west toward the Santa Fe, California, and Oregon trails, the Missouri River saw high amounts of traffic. Thanks to the river, Kansas City exists today.

Originally, the population at Chouteau's trading post consisted of Native Americans, fur trappers, French settlers, and slaves. But as westward expansion increased in the United States, pioneers streamed into the area, and with them came diversity. The river drew bargainers who came to trade with Native Americans, and traders who met travelers from the Santa Fe trail to purchase their goods. The Santa Fe trail brought Mexicans to the area. The California and Oregon trails attracted immigrant pioneer groups headed west. The livelihood of the Town of Kansas depended on these travelers and traders, and hotels sprung up along the Missouri River's bluffs. All the passersby and immigrants profoundly shaped the nature of the early city.

Kansas City and How It Grew describes the effects on the neighboring town, Independence: "Residents also began to experience a society more diverse than they had ever imagined." The river brought both good and bad to the city. It brought trade and profit; it brought missionaries and Christianity. However, it also brought robbers, illegal trade, and corruption. *Kansas City and How It Grew* states of Independence, Missouri, "According to one account from the period: 'Mexicans, Californians, and strangers from every state in the union find their way thither. Among such a motley multitude, there is much of human nature to be seen.'" As the main trade hub transitioned to the Town of Kansas instead of Independence, the same could be said of Kansas City.

Mormon Migration

In the early 1830s, the river brought another group: the Mormons. Mormonism began in upstate New York in 1830 when twenty-four-year-old Joseph Smith founded the Church of Jesus Christ of Latter-day Saints, claiming a revelation from God had given him the Book of Mormon. After receiving persecution in New York and then Ohio, Smith brought his followers to Jackson County, Missouri, where he believed Zion to be. The Mormons settled, but coming from the North, they brought their abolitionist sentiments with them, which were not well received among neighboring Missouri settlers—nor were their elitist claims of being the only true church.

In 1833, the Mormon newspaper, *The Evening and the Morning Star*, published an abolitionist article. Missouri was a slave state, and the article kindled locals' already smoldering anti-Mormon sentiments. The article resulted in local residents destroying the Mormons' newspaper press, driving some Mormons from their homes, and tarring two of their leaders. The Mormons relocated farther north in Clay County. Hostility continued, and five years later in 1838, Missouri Governor Lilburn Boggs ordered the Mormons to be "exterminated or driven from the state." That winter, ten thousand Mormons migrated back east to Nauvoo, Illinois.

The abolitionist sentiments of the Mormons were but small sparks in the larger storm that was to engulf the nation in the form of the Civil War.

Built on Generosity

Looking at our history, we can see the grit of real life—a city that celebrated slavery and ran the Mormons out of town. A businessman who cheated on an auction and swindled land owners. A flood that wiped out an entire business district. By no means were Kansas City's early days a perfect, rosy era.

Yet kindness shone through trials, and righteousness rose to the top. The early leaders of Kansas City lived lives of generosity and self-sacrifice. McCoy gave up his personal possessions for John Sutter, and although only that one instance made the history books, you can be sure it wasn't the first time he was generous. That act sprang from a lifestyle of generosity. Similarly, Berenice Chouteau gave sacrificially. She sacrificed her time and energy to visit the Native American villages and care for their sick. Likewise, Dr. Nathan Scarritt also sacrificed, giving from his personal fortune to build a Bible school and a missionary training school.

From its start, Kansas City was rooted in giving. The leaders' faith impacted their lives and led them to give sacrificially. Their generosity shaped the character of our city and left a legacy for us to follow.

Chapter 3
The Civil War Splits the Church

...

(1850 – 1870)

Off Tenth and Broadway in the Quality Hill neighborhood stands the Coates House Hotel, a narrow, six-story brick building now renamed Quality Hill Condominiums and Apartments. The hotel is nestled in a bustling neighborhood marked by tall brick buildings and a scenic view of the river below. Though now surrounded by cars and passersby, this residence started as a lonely structure next to a fort during the Civil War. Kersey Coates laid its foundation a year before the Civil War and paused construction during the war. Union troops boarded over the unfinished hotel foundation and used it for cavalry barns. After the war ended and the horses no longer needed the foundation, Coates resumed construction on the hotel. Walking into the building today, its interior glows white—floors, walls, furniture, lamps—all a shining contrast to its rugged beginnings. Coates and his wife Sarah played a pivotal role in Kansas City's church during the Civil War. In order to understand the Coates' role, we must take a step back and study Kansas City and America during the decades leading up to the war.

In the mid-1800s, a spiritual revival known as the Second Great Awakening broke out in both Europe and America. Protestant revivalism swept across America, including Kansas City. The great theologians and preachers traveled the country and held revivals and camp meetings. In the years leading up to the Civil War, Kansas City had its own share of meetings. Audiences traveled by wagons, horseback, and carts to attend the services that occurred day and night.

Edward Scarritt, son of Dr. Nathan Scarritt, recalled his experience with one such meeting in the late 1850s: "It was a regular and continuous whirlwind of religious oratory and onslaught on Satan's forces from the beginning of the campaign till the end of the week." Audience members camped at the revival sites and cooked potatoes, cabbage, corn, and corned beef. Scarritt remembers as a boy appreciating the "pies, cakes, cookies, ginger bread, puddings and other like things [which] were cooked at home and were there in abundance." The preaching continued the entire week long, and Scarritt wrote, "When one exhorter became weary or fell from the ranks, another was in readiness to take his place." This camp revival occurred just a few years before the Civil War.

The revivals and the Second Great Awakening heightened the nation's moral conscience, which caused mounting tension as citizens debated slavery's acceptability. Many Americans grew increasingly convicted that God had created all people equally, including slaves. However, the South's economy depended on slavery. The South insisted that because of each state's autonomy, each should be able to decide its own laws regarding slavery. Hence the tensions arose that would culminate in the Civil War.

Fighting for Freedom

Before Kansas gained statehood, the US government left Kansas up for grabs regarding whether it would enter the union as a slave state or as a free state. People from Missouri, a slave state, crossed the border into Kansas to try to make it another slave state. At the same time, abolitionists traveled from the northern states to try to make it a free state.

Kersey Coates and Sarah Coates, were city leaders and Quakers who fought for abolition in Kansas.

Enter Sarah and Kersey Coates—strong Christians and staunch abolitionists. Sarah Coates grew up in Pennsylvania watching the Disciples of Christ preachers. Her father told the story of Sarah as a little girl standing outside and preaching to the chickens. The chickens never converted, but her little sermons were a precursor to her strong convictions and her heart to serve people and preach the truth.

Sarah and Kersey Coates (seated right) on the front porch of their home with their four children.

At age fifteen Sarah wrote in her diary, "When can I do something to relieve the oppressed of our land? My spirit mourns when I think of the apathy that is manifested by so large a number in relation to breaking bonds of enslavement." A staunch abolitionist from a young age, Sarah's passions followed her into adulthood.

> "When can I do something to relieve the oppressed of our land?"
>
> -Sarah Coates

Sarah's family moved from Pennsylvania to Kansas in 1854, the year Congress passed the Kansas-Nebraska Act. This act allowed both territories to decide for themselves whether they would be slave or free, and as a result, abolitionists flooded to Kansas to try to make it a free state. At the same time, Kersey Coates moved to Kansas City as well. Kersey and Sarah met and then married two years later. Together, they were a power couple. They shared their Quaker faith along with their abolitionist stance. They "were eager participants in the Free State movement, helping settle Kansas Territory as a state free from slavery." They helped settlers move to the Kansas

Territory to end slavery there. As newlyweds, they lived in the Gilliss House Hotel and during the uproar of bleeding Kansas, *The Kansas City Spirit* records, "Here Sarah Coates provided a hiding spot for the first territorial governor of Kansas, Andrew H. Reeder, who was fleeing the pro-slavery faction that was looking to shoot him on sight. She hid him away for two weeks before he was able to make his way to the river and a flatboat headed for the safety of Chicago."

The Coates were strong abolitionists, and they were also religious. There were not enough Quakers in the area to constitute their own church, so the Coates helped found the All Souls Unitarian Church, which remains active today. After the war, Sarah organized the first Women's Christian Association in 1870, a group of Protestant women who set out to help impoverished women and children in town. Sarah wrote of the children's home they opened, "Our home became the recipient of all classes of distressed humanity, and especially did unfortunate children pour in upon us, and it was thus that the Children's Home came into existence."

Kansas City was already a small town to begin with when the Civil War started, and it continued to struggle during the war. It essentially became a war post as soldiers traveled through. During the Civil War, Kersey served as a colonel in the Missouri Militia. He had just laid the foundation for the Coates House Hotel, and he turned the structure into a stable to serve the Union Cavalry during the war.

Both Sarah and Kersey played significant roles in fighting for freedom during the Civil War, and they would continue to hold a prominent place in Kansas City society for years to come.

Churches Torn Apart

In Kansas City, the nationwide division was reflected in the church roster even before the Civil War began. Two years before the war, an 1859 directory of Kansas City lists seven churches:
1. Baptist
2. Catholic (led by Rev. Bernard Donnelly)
3. Episcopal
4. Methodist (South)
5. Methodist (North)
6. Presbyterian (First)
7. Reformed Church (Disciples of Christ)

The labels for the two Methodist churches were not based on geography. They did not indicate which churches were on the north and south sides of Kansas City. Rather, these divisions show that the Methodist church denomination had split into two sects over the issue of slavery. The Methodist's northern division sided with the Union, and the southern division sided with the Confederacy. The Baptist church would soon follow.

First Baptist Church of Kansas City began just six years before the Civil War. It opened under the leadership of Lykins, who also helped McCoy lead a Baptist mission to the Shawnee. The church's history describes its first several years as "a struggle, for the flock was small, the people were nearly all poor, and they had no permanent house in which to hold services . . ." They finally scraped together enough funds to build a building, but when their pastor, R. S. Thomas, preached his first sermon in the new building, that sermon ended up also being his last. Thomas became sick and died shortly afterwards. A new pastor served one year, then the Civil War began, and "the flock was scattered." The church ceased meeting for the first three years of the war, until Dr. Jonathan B. Fuller came on as their third pastor. Fuller was born in Scotland and came to the United States at age eight. After becoming an ordained minister, he moved to Kansas City at age twenty-four to pastor First Baptist Church. He moved in with Lykins's family and refused to let the war keep the fledgling church from meeting. The church's history states, "Once during a revival meeting, [Fuller] refused to bow to the war and continued his revival meeting even as guns were being fired in the battle of Westport."

Though Fuller did his best to lead the church, the congregation held split views. Fuller sided with the Union, as did many members of his church. However, other members had sons fighting on the Confederate side. By 1866, his church officially split over sectional differences. Fuller led the Northern-sympathizing group from First Baptist to open Walnut Street Church, later known as Central Church. It was not until seven years after the Civil War that the two Baptist churches decided to reunite. First Baptist Church of Kansas City continues today off Red Bridge Road and Wornall Road in South Kansas City. Though the church

> "He continued his revival meeting even as guns were being fired in the battle of Westport."

eventually reunited, its division echoed what was happening with the nation as a whole.

Many churches closed their doors as Kansas City became an occupied city. Missouri was pro-slavery, but so many abolitionists like the Coates had immigrated from the North to Kansas City, they were able to elect a mayor who sided with the Union—Robert Van Horn. Threatened by Confederate presence, Van Horn ordered the exile of anyone living on the outskirts of Kansas City "who could not establish their loyalty to the satisfaction of Army authorities," according to *Kansas City: An American Story*. Over sixty people were removed, including John Calvin McCoy, the Father of Kansas City, who relocated to Glasgow, Missouri. Van Horn brought in two hundred Union soldiers, and Kansas City became a war outpost for the Union Army. One newspaper stated that every citizen "carried arms and slept with revolvers under their pillows."

The war affected every aspect of life—families fought against each other, businesses shut down, neighborhoods were ransacked, and churches struggled to survive. The first Episcopal church, Saint Mary's Church, was young—only three years old when the Union occupation began. The church struggled to maintain a presence in the city, and *The Early History of Greater Kansas City* records that the church went on hiatus "at the beginning of the war, when the members became scattered and regular services were suspended for a period of nearly four years."

Then and Now
Though the church closed its doors for a season during the Civil War, Saint Mary's Episcopal Church remains today in downtown Kansas City at the corner of Thirteenth and Holmes.

Brave Beginnings
Kansas City churches responded to the war in different ways. Some churches split. Some closed their doors during the war. Still others took the war as an opportunity to increase evangelism or even to begin new churches.

The First Congregational Church started meeting during the Civil War with a small crowd of only seven people. Hoggins writes, "While virtually every church in Kansas City was disorganized and its place of worship abandoned on account of the Civil War, the nucleus of the First Congregational group was formed . . ." Kansas City, at the time, was a military outpost of only about five thousand people. Dr. Henry Hopkins, a later pastor of the church, recounted the church's first meeting:

> In the summer of 1863, while the war was on, when this was a military post, and the only safe road out of it was toward Wyandotte, brethren from Kansas hired Long's Hall [a local hall in Kansas City] and, crossing the Kaw by ferry, came through the forest on the West Bottoms and held, on Sunday morning, a preaching service.

Although their first service began humbly, the small congregation slowly grew, eventually becoming a passionate church that would greatly influence Kansas City in the years to come. Some of Kansas City's greatest leaders and most famous names would come out of this church. Out of its roots of chaos and war came a church full of dedication and devotion to both God and to the city.

> *"While virtually every church in Kansas City was disorganized and its place of worship abandoned on account of the Civil War, the nucleus of First Congregational group was formed . . ."*

Stragglers Camp and African American Churches

At the same time, after Abraham Lincoln's Emancipation Proclamation, many freed slaves fled the south and traveled up the Missouri River toward Kansas, a free state. They stopped and camped on the banks of the river, so black preachers in Kansas City started holding revival meetings down by the river. In the typical style of nineteenth-century revivals, Rev. Clark Moore started a mission known as Stragglers Camp near the Missouri River. Crowds gathered to listen to him preach, and the ferry's steamboat whistles intermingled with the singing from late night worship services. One Sunday, they held their largest revival yet. As audience members were baptized, Moore asked them to choose which church they wanted to join by walking to either the leader of the Baptist church or the leader of the Methodist church. Today, if you go to the website of Second Baptist Church, you can read its story:

> Assisted by a Reverend Mr. Lovelace, the Reverend Mr. Moore gave each convert the opportunity to express his choice of denomination affiliation: Baptist or Methodist. Two-thirds of the attending group decided to unite as Baptist [and] one-third as Methodist. These two groups were then known and have since been known as Second Baptist and Alien Chapel A.M.E. [African Methodist Episcopal].

These two churches, still alive today, are the two oldest African American churches in Kansas City.

The community of black believers regularly held baptisms at Brush Creek. One onlooker wrote, "The Negro slaves were even more fervent in their revivals and more picturesque [than their white counterparts]. They were always looking for miracles, and their faith was wonderfully rewarded, according to their own testimony."

> "They were always looking for miracles, and their faith was wonderfully rewarded . . ."

Churches at the Battle of Westport

Fear increased in 1864 as rumors spread that the Confederate Major General Sterling Price's troops were marching toward Kansas City. Having failed to seize St. Louis, Price was now heading further west. Union troops began patrolling Kansas City's streets each night, tying their horses in the Baptist churchyard to graze.

The rumors proved true. Confederate troops arrived on Saturday, October 22, while Fuller was holding his Baptist revival service. *Kansas City: An American Story* records, "That night, at a revival in Westport, Fuller saw the Rebel watch fires burning a few miles south. He went to bed 'in the rather uncomfortable conviction that the first glimmer of daylight would find the Rebels in our streets.'"

The following Sunday morning, battle ensued. Troops met just south of Brush Creek. One soldier, William Sidney Shepherd, later recalled,

> The day of the battle 'was warm, warm from the sun, the burning grass and haycocks and the excitement of roaring cannon and rifle fire. . . The church bells did not ring, although it was Sunday. People of Westport were too busy serving Union soldiers and worrying whether the Confederates would win and sack the town. On that day Kansas City was besieged. What now is the Country Club Plaza was peppered with cannon balls.'

Union troops won the battle, and the Southern army retreated. The battle ended by late afternoon, and the whole town went out to survey the damage. They counted fifteen hundred soldiers dead. After the battle of Westport, Confederate troops retreated south, where they lost another battle in Mine Creek, Kansas, and then eventually retreated into Arkansas and then Texas.

Although church bells did not ring that day, the church busied itself caring for the sick. The Methodist Episcopal Church, South, converted into a makeshift hospital. Wounded soldiers lined its pews, lying head to toe covered in white sheets and blankets, row after row. Dr. Scarritt's wife served as one of many volunteer nurses. Her son Edward Scarritt, eleven at the time, accompanied her and remembers hearing the soldiers' moans as nurses tended to the wounds until he finally "crawled up into the pulpit and went to sleep." Once again, Kansas City's churches were at the forefront of the action, guiding the city through difficult times.

Truth at Any Cost

During the Civil War, Kansas City's churches brought light during a dark time. As some churches closed their doors during the Civil War, new churches emerged—churches that carried the torch of Christianity during the war. Many African Americans came to Christ during the Stragglers' Camp Revival and started two new churches. Likewise, the First Congregational Church began during the war. The Baptist church persevered in meeting despite gunshots ringing out from the Battle of Westport. Hard times tested the churches and revealed churches' true character. The war forced them to determine who they were and what they stood for.

The Civil War tested the churches, yet one must also ask whether churches caused the Civil War. At its heart, the war sprung from the moral issue of slavery. It followed on the heels of America's Second Great Awakening. As the country woke up to spirituality, slavery pricked its conscience. Northerners hated slavery, yet Southerners' economy depended on it. Slavery was a moral, economical, and political issue that proved explosive. In the end, both the churches and the nation itself divided over the issue.

On a miniature scale, churches did what President Lincoln would not allow the nation to do—divide. The South wanted the United States to part ways, agree to disagree, and become two independent nations. Yet Lincoln said, "No, we're staying united *and* we're ending slavery, no matter the cost." Churches, however, did not take this route. They divided, shut down, or formed new churches that were one-sided.

Churches' responses to the Civil War hold valuable lessons for us today. We must determine whether moral issues are worth fighting for. At what cost will we stand up for what we believe? What if other Christians disagree? We must decide when to fight for unity, when to divide, and when to reconcile after a division.

As the war came to a close and the city found itself in shambles, churches rose up to reconcile a broken city and shape its destiny.

Chapter 4

Growth through Diversity

...

(1869 – 1915)

Just years before the Civil War, the little Town of Kansas had been renamed the City of Kansas (quickly shortened to "Kansas City"). As the war ended, Kansas City found itself a destroyed city trying to recover from the Battle of Westport and the chaos of the war. Deep animosity lay between Kansas and Missouri from the decades of state line battles between the free-state Jayhawkers from Kansas and the pro-slavery bushwhackers from Missouri. (Even the University of Kansas received its mascot from these skirmishes between the two states, and a friendly rivalry continues to this day between the University of Missouri and the University of Kansas.) Kansas City took the brunt of the two states' conflict, since the state line sliced the city in half. Although Missouri never joined the Confederacy, it identified as a slave state, and its citizens had fought hard before the war to make Kansas a slave state as well. After the Civil War, as Kansas City grew from a quiet, poky town into a bustling city, its leaders felt the need to reestablish trust between citizens whose loyalties had pitted them against each other in the Civil War.

A Bridge to the Future

Now that the war had ended, Kersey Coates and the other city leaders needed new direction. They had stood for abolition, joined with the Union, fought, and won the Civil War. Now what? Not only did Kansas City need to rebuild from the wreckage, but the small town also found itself needing to build, period. It had not been a large city, and its leaders were trying to establish a vision of what the city would become in the years ahead. They decided to devote their energies into reuniting Kansas City and building it into a major city. The first step was to get a railroad to come through town.

But there was a problem. A big, muddy river lay between Kansas City and the rest of civilization—St. Louis, Chicago, and the eastern cities. For a railroad to come to Kansas City, the city would first have to build a bridge over the Missouri River—a daunting task for a small town. The city leaders devised an architectural plan for building a bridge across the Missouri. Battling against the river's deep, muddy bottom, they didn't know how far down they would have to sink the bridge's foundations before they hit bedrock. But they decided to try.

After two years of construction, they completed the Hannibal Bridge. An 1869 *Kansas City Times* article said, "We succeeded because we were not torn by factions growing out of local jealousies." The article attributed the success in securing the bridge

> "We succeeded because we were not torn by factions..."
>
> -Kansas City Times

to "a united, harmonious and public-spirited community." The bridge served as a sign of the city's recovery and move toward unity. Throughout Kansas City's history, Christians like Kersey Coates did much to invest in the future of the city. Their faith encompassed more than church, and they saw God's will as intertwined with the good of the city.

The railway system connected Kansas City from the southwest cattle herders in Texas, Colorado, and Kansas all the way up to the northern cities of Chicago, New York, and anywhere else in the eastern United States. Now Kansas City had achieved a spot on the map.

Then and Now
Today, driving south on Interstate 29 toward the heart of downtown Kansas City, just before you cross the Missouri River, you will see a sign marking the exit for Armour Road. This road on the north side of the city earned its name from the Armour family, who helped turn Kansas City into a booming city.

Armour Road cuts across North Kansas City and earned its name from the Armour family's legacy.

Cowtown Begins
The completion of the Hannibal Bridge opened the way for new commerce. After the bridge was built, the Armour family came from Chicago to start a meatpacking plant in Kansas City. First, Philip Armour moved here, then his brothers, Simeon Armour and Andrew Armour, joined him. Andrew's sons, Kirkland Armour and Charles Armour, came as well. They opened Kansas City's first meatpacking house, and they prospered from their slaughterhouses. With the railroad catering to the newly forming

beef industry, Kansas City became a cow town. The ranchers herded their cattle from Texas, Colorado, and Kansas up to Kansas City, the end of the line for the herders.

Once the cattle reached the West Bottoms of Kansas City, they were slaughtered, then the meat was packaged in meatpacking plants and shipped by train across the country. On a warm summer day, residents could smell the blood from the meatpacking plants. Residents called the stench "the smell of money." Thanks to its slaughterhouses and meatpacking plants, Kansas City became a major center for the meat industry nationwide—the largest city between San Francisco and St. Louis.

Simeon B. Armour and his wife Margaret opened Armour meat packing and used their fortune to build homes for orphans and the elderly.

A postcard of Armour Packing Co. depicts the meatpacking plants that earned Kansas City a spot in the nation's economy.

DISCOVERING THE PAST TO SHAPE OUR FUTURE

Next to their personal home, the Armours built a home for orphans (building on left).

    Though the history annals never explicitly state the Armours' faith, one can surmise that they were Christian from the legacy that Margaret Armour left Kansas City. Margaret Armour served as president of the Women's Christian Association for nearly twenty-five years. *The Kansas City Spirit* records, "William A. Slater, former managing executive director of WCA, wrote that three important forces guided Mrs. Armour: commitment, deep religious beliefs, and 'a sense of noblesse oblige, a sense of recognizing her blessing and wanting to help others less fortunate in the best sense.'" Margaret and her husband, Simeon, started a home for orphans and a home for the elderly, and they donated large amounts from their personal fortune toward each home.

    As the city recovered from the Civil War, so did the churches. At the beginning of the war, Kansas City claimed only seven churches. After the war, churches in Kansas City more than doubled. Thirteen new churches formed during the first five years after the Civil War, bringing the total number of churches up to twenty. Sadly, while churches in Kansas City multiplied, they did not keep up with the explosive population growth resulting from the building of the Hannibal Bridge and the coming of the railroad. Just before the Civil War, the United States Census showed four thousand people, and a city directory listed seven churches—one for every six hundred people. Ten years later, the population had grown to over thirty-two thousand, yet there were only twenty churches, or one for every sixteen hundred people. The church had its work cut out for it.

THE SPIRITUAL ROOTS OF KANSAS CITY

In 1882, Westport Baptist Church persuaded its pastor, William T. Campbell, to resign his pastorate and become a missionary to Kansas City, trying to establish a church in a new section of the city. All over the city, church leaders were reaching out and forming new churches.

Exodusters Seek Refuge

One major group to immigrate to Kansas City after the Civil War was the Exodusters, former slaves who sought to start a new life in Kansas. As Kansas City rebuilt from the war, much of the nation was doing the same. Although the former slaves had technically gained freedom, they still faced animosity in the South. In 1877, reconstruction efforts ended, and the South became increasingly hostile to former slaves. A minority report commissioned by the US Senate in 1879 stated that the black migrants left the South "because they were unable to endure the intolerable hardships, injustice and suffering inflicted upon them by the Democrats of the South, [and] fled panic stricken from their homes and sought refuge in a strange land."

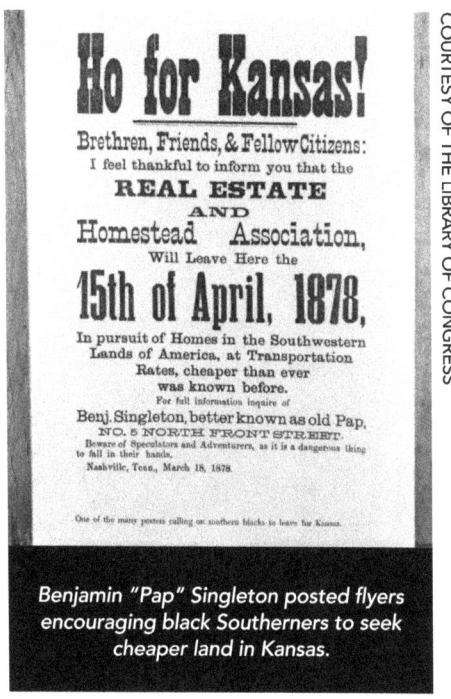

Rumors spread throughout the South that there was free land for the taking in Kansas. If migrants could only make it upriver, they could claim the land. Many former slaves from southern states migrated toward Kansas, hoping to find racial equality in an abolitionist state. Benjamin "Pap" Singleton organized thousands of migrants who became known as the Exodusters. They traveled up the Mississippi River in steamboats and then up the Missouri River, propelled by the hope of a new life once they reached the clear blue skies and the golden grain fields of Kansas.

Thousands of former slaves came with nothing except the fare to pay for the ferry to take them upriver. They traveled upriver and

Benjamin "Pap" Singleton posted flyers encouraging black Southerners to seek cheaper land in Kansas.

Former slaves, known as "Exodusters," migrated to Kansas as refugees, and thousands settled in Kansas City.

landed in St. Louis. Most of them were broke. In a thesis on the migration, Lee Ella Blake reports that fifteen hundred black migrants landed in St. Louis in February and March of 1879, but St. Louis did not allow them to stay. A few hundred migrants who could afford the fare traveled on to Kansas City. The rest were broke and in St. Louis—hundreds of people sitting homeless by the ferry.

One reporter walked up to an Exoduster and asked, "How are you going to make it through?"

The Exoduster replied, "The good Lord will see us safe through. . . . He's got us all in the hollow of His hand and He'll fetch us through to Kansas or the Promised Land all in His own time." They had the same faith as the Hebrews in the first Exodus, who set out from Egypt not knowing where they were going or what their provision would be. As freed slaves, they had nothing except a trust that the Lord would carry them through.

St. Louis did not want the migrants there, so some city leaders secretly paid the fare to get them out of St. Louis and back on the ferry to Kansas City.

THE SPIRITUAL ROOTS OF KANSAS CITY

In early April 1879, the steamboat Fannie Lewis chugged into Kansas City "towing two barges on which were crowded 1,000 Negro refugees . . ." and landed on the riverbank in Wyandotte County. Like St. Louis, the citizens of Kansas City objected to them landing. Corvine Patterson, a Baptist deacon and former slave, along with W. J. Buchan, a white state senator and former Union soldier, convinced the city leaders to let them stay. Blake writes, "Fires were built on the river bank, and the Negroes prepared their supper from viands furnished by generous citizens to accompaniment of such spirituals as 'Rock Daniel,' 'Ride on Jesus, Ride On,' and 'I've Done Got Over.'" They congregated by the river and set up camp, forming tent villages in Wyandotte County. In the following weeks, Simeon B. Armour and his brother Philip D. Armour, who themselves had recently immigrated to Kansas City from Chicago, contributed wagonloads of food to the refugees.

> "The good Lord will see us safe through . . ."
>
> -Exoduster

As the weeks went by, more steamboats kept dropping off hundreds of Exodusters, until the refugees' numbers climbed over two thousand. Kansas City, Kansas, gave rations of bread and meat to them. However, as Exodusters continued to arrive, the city feared that it would soon be bankrupt. City leaders debated what to do. They couldn't support a pop-up homeless population of thousands of people. They decided to ferry some of them farther upriver to the cities of Atchison, Leavenworth, Lawrence, Manhattan, and other towns in Kansas. Over the next few years, the city of St. Louis estimated fifteen thousand Exodusters passing through on their way to Kansas City, Leavenworth, and Topeka.

Those who stayed in Kansas City, Kansas, set up squatters' shanties out of scrap wood and found employment in the railroads, factories, and meatpacking houses of the West Bottoms. The tent villagers gradually blended into Kansas City's African American community and churches on the north end of the city.

International Churches Emerge

On the tail of the Exodusters, immigrants from around the world began streaming to Kansas City. Nationwide, the industrial revolution drew millions of immigrant workers to the United States, and Kansas City received its share. The city experienced explosive growth after the Civil War up through 1915. As different people groups immigrated to Kansas City in search of work, they each brought their unique faith with them. Thankfully, the churches rose up to meet this challenge of a growing city.

With the massive immigration in the early twentieth century, the Catholic Church adapted to the changes. In 1880 the Vatican decided to form the Diocese of Kansas City, naming John Joseph Hogan the founding bishop. Two years later, Bishop Hogan went on to establish the Cathedral of the Immaculate Conception at Eleventh and Broadway, the same spot where the Chouteaus' original church stood. Catholic parishes, hospitals, and homes expanded in Kansas City and the surrounding areas.

Bishop John Joseph Hogan initiated construction on the Cathedral of the Immaculate Conception to serve the city's growing Catholic population. The cathedral stands today in the same spot as the city's first parish, "Chouteau's Church."

During the 1880s and 1890s, many Italian masons immigrated with their families. The city imported labor for marble and stone masonry, both for the construction of the Catholic diocese and for other buildings in Kansas City. Today you can still see the ornate stonework on the Catholic Diocese and the buildings next to it off Ninth and Baltimore—landmarks to their craftmanship. The Italians stayed in the city, and with their presence grew Catholicism. Italian Scalabrini missionaries came to serve the Italian immigrants, and they established Holy Rosary Parish in the north end.

Along with the immigration of Italians and Sicilians, other ethnicities entered the city as well. Irish immigrants increased in numbers, strengthening the presence of Irish Catholicism. Polish immigrants worked in Kansas City's stockyard and started St. Stanislaus Parish, a Polish church. Monsignor Ernest Zechenter arrived in Kansas City from Germany and immediately established St. Peter and Paul Catholic Church, Kansas City's first German Catholic Church. The start of the 1900s found Catholicism well established in the city.

Each immigrant group spurred a startup church for its own nationality. Many workers from the southern part of Europe were recruited around the turn of the century to work in the meatpacking houses. They settled in the West Bottoms, but the 1903 flood displaced them, forcing them to move upland across the Kansas River to an area known as Strawberry Hill. Swedish immigrants settled on the west side of the city and Jewish immigrants on the east side. When Russian-Germans immigrated to Kansas City seeking religious freedom and farmland, they brought with them their Mennonite faith.

While meatpacking companies recruited from Europe, railroad companies recruited from Mexico. Between 1910 and 1920, over two thousand Mexicans immigrated to Kansas City. In 1925 they started the city's first predominantly Mexican church, Our Lady of Mount Carmel. By 1937, Kansas City had churches for Mexicans, Croatians, Germans, Greeks, Irish, Lithuanians, Mexicans, Poles, Russians, Serbians, Slovakians, and Slovenians.

A City of Refuge

The close of the Civil War brought an era of growth and healing for Kansas City. The Hannibal Bridge, completed just four years after the war, brought two sides together, both literally and symbolically. Factions that had been divided during the war now learned to work together on a project that would benefit the city.

In Timothy Keller's "Theology of Cities", he explains how God intended cities as places of protection and safety. The Old Testament law designated literal "cities of refuge." If someone accidentally killed a neighbor, they could flee to a city of refuge and be safe from anyone seeking to avenge the death. Throughout history, the very walls of a city offered protection from enemies. The higher population density offered strength in numbers and shelter for the weak. Today, although cities don't have literal walls, they still offer protection for the vulnerable through the form of government services offered in cities and through people who can look out for those in need.

In the years following the Civil War, Kansas City became a city of refuge for refugees and immigrants. When thousands of Exodusters migrated up the Mississippi and Missouri Rivers, escaping a hostile South, God provided Kansas City as a place of protection, provision, and a new start at life. The city gave the Exodusters jobs or transportation to other cities up the Kansas River. By no means does Kansas City have a spotless record of caring for minorities, as we will see in the chapters ahead. But this was one shining moment in our history.

Perhaps immigrants found refuge because the leaders who spoke up for them had been in similar spots. Corvine Patterson, the Baptist deacon who helped convince the city to let the Exodusters stay, had himself been a slave earlier in life. He could relate to their plight. Senator Buchan had enlisted as a Union soldier nearly twenty years earlier, and his fight for freedom did not end when the war came to a close. He continued to speak out on former slaves' behalf. Similarly, the Armour family had recently arrived in Kansas City, and as they handed out food at refugee camps on the riverbank, they could likely relate to being strangers in town, longing to be taken in. For the Exodusters and other immigrant populations who followed in the years afterward, Kansas City became a city of refuge. As the city's population increased, it would also need to become a city of beauty.

Chapter 5

Dreamers Build the City

...

(1880 – 1921)

One by one, churches in Kansas City sprang up from individuals who could dream. Church historian Olive Hoggins tells the story of one such dreamer: "Mrs. T. C. Cox, with her baby, lay in a hammock, under the trees, on the hills, busy regaining her health. She dreamed a dream of a Baptist community, united and working in harmony in a church on this hill. There was no church, no houses, no people, only staked off lots and mud." In her freshly built neighborhood, Mrs. Cox started Bible studies and prayer meetings in homes in the spring of 1912. She gathered women to canvas their neighborhood for a new church. Hoggins writes, "The women went out two and two and dragged through the mud, calling on every family in the sparsely settled community, creating interest in the work and inviting people to the meetings. Mr. and Mrs. Cox contracted for the lot and mortgaged their own little home for the lumber for a small one-room chapel. Mrs. Cox decorated it herself." This story of Mrs. Cox shows the determination of early Christians in Kansas City and their initiative to spark religious change.

Then and Now
Have you ever traversed the winding paths of the Kansas City Zoo? Or watched a show in Starlight Theatre? Have you driven past Hyde Park or the Country Club District? None of these trademarks of Kansas City would exist if not for First Congregational Church and its pastor, Rev. Dr. Henry Hopkins, who had a vision for what would become known as the City Beautiful Movement.

The City Beautiful Movement
Remember how we noted in chapter three that the First Congregational Church, born during the Civil War, would grow up to be a very influential church in Kansas City? Well, the late nineteenth century was its time to shine.

An early pastor of First Congregational Church, Rev. J. G. Roberts wrote in a letter, "The church was a missionary church, and Kansas City was a wild, rough place, the headquarters of all the gamblers of the plains." Rebuilding from the Civil War, Kansas City fell far short of the city we know and love today. It boasted no fountains,

> "The church was a missionary church, and Kansas City was a wild, rough place . . ."
>
> -Rev. J. G. Roberts

DISCOVERING THE PAST TO SHAPE OUR FUTURE

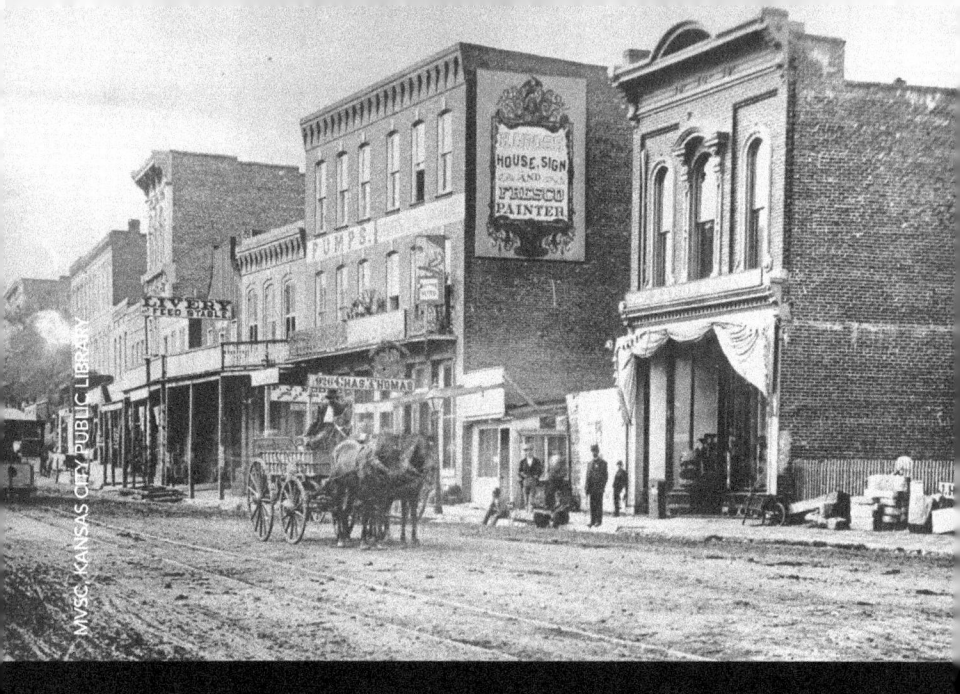

Dirt roads lined downtown Kansas City in the late 1800s.

no sweeping boulevards, no sprawling parks. Instead, Kansas City stood as a messy conglomeration of dirt roads and ramshackle buildings placed haphazardly at builders' whims. The river, trains, and trailheads created a boisterous cow town full of pioneers heading west, cowboys herding cattle, and travelers entering from every corner of the United States. Writer Charles Gleed observed that post-Civil-War Kansas City

> was a sight to make granite eyes shed tears... The population of the city included as fine a collection of ruffian brotherhood and sisterhood of the wild West as could be well imagined. Renegade Indians, demoralized soldiers, unreformed bushwhackers, and border ruffians, thieves, and thugs imported from anywhere, professional train robbers of home growth, and all kinds of wrecks from the Civil War.

The city's landscaping reflected its citizens, and it wasn't the prettiest town to live in.

But First Congregational Church had a vision for Kansas City to become more. Following Rev. Roberts, a new pastor arrived: Rev. Dr.

Built near the river, Kansas City's buildings perched on top of bluffs, with graded roads leading down to the river.

Henry Hopkins. He started pastoring First Congregational Church, the stalwart church born during the dark days of the Civil War which had grown to become one of the largest churches in town. Hopkins began pastoring in 1880. Thirty years later, the church published a book of its history, stating,

> From this moment, with Henry Hopkins as pastor ... the church went steadily forward, increasing in numbers and influence until it became one of the strong centers of religious life in the city, not only for Congregationalists, but in a sense, for all denominations, so strong a personal hold did Dr. Hopkins gain upon all who were interested in the moral and spiritual betterment of Kansas City.

Hopkins saw a bigger vision for what the city could become, and he used his pulpit to change the course of the city. Hoggins wrote, "It was during the ministry of Dr. Hopkins that the big overgrown cowboy town began to take on a new civic consciousness and become a real city." Hopkins firmly believed that the Christian faith should affect every area of life. It should not be contained within the four walls of a church one day of the week but should infiltrate all of society. The book *A Brief History of the First Congregational Church* records his sermon on how the church should impact a city:

> The growing thought now, is . . . to embody [Christ] in all the activities of all the seven days, to become a part of the times in which we live, a potent factor for Christ's sake, in the advancing history of the world, in the beneficent movements of reform; to make the Gospel felt in municipal government, in jurisprudence and legislature, in education and art and literature; in commerce and the great world of industry, and in all the complex forms of our associated activity . . . that the kingdom of heaven for whose coming we pray is to come in this world.

He preached a sermon declaring God's design for cities to become beautiful. His sermon caused such a stir that he put it into a booklet form as well. This began the City Beautiful movement.

August R. Meyer, who came to be called the Father of Kansas City's park system, belonged to Hopkins's church. The Kessler Society of Kansas City describes Meyer as "an ideal type of nineteenth-century businessman. A European-educated multimillionaire, he possessed a rich personality that combined enthusiasm, gentility, and charm." Hopkins's sermon deeply inspired Meyer. He formed Kansas City's first park board and served as president on the board. Four of the five members of

August R. Meyer became "the father of Kansas City's park system" after being inspired by his pastor's sermons on "the City Beautiful."

the park board were also members of First Congregational Church: August R. Meyer, Adriance Van Brunt, Robert Gillham, and J. K. Burnham. They lived out the sermon in a tangible way and forever changed Kansas City.

The committee hired George Kessler to design park and boulevard systems for Kansas City. Kessler remained committed to working on the park system even when other companies offered him larger salaries. Hoggins wrote of Kessler, "When he had opportunity to abandon the work for a larger salary he refused, deeming the completion of this work 'greater riches than the treasures of Egypt.'" Kessler designed Hyde Park, the Country Club District, and numerous other parks and boulevards. He developed an "interlocking system of parks and boulevards [that] enhanced virtually all elements of urban life . . ."

> *"When he had opportunity to abandon the work for a larger salary he refused, deeming the completion of this work 'greater riches than the treasures of Egypt.'"*

Hopkins's sermon also inspired another landowner—Thomas Swope. Swope gifted thirteen hundred acres for Swope Park. At the time, his donation was the largest land donation for a park in history. As Hoggins observed, "[T]he fact that Swope park is the joy of thousands of children today, is due to the inspirational leadership of this great preacher."

Then and Now

Today Swope Park remains one of the largest urban parks in the United States. It hosts the Kansas City Zoo, Starlight Theatre, a golf course, community gardens, a pool, a training facility for Sporting KC, and other community resources. Thomas Swope, along with the rest of the city, worked hard to build into Kansas City the park system and beautiful places we enjoy today.

The City Beautiful movement elevated Kansas City to national recognition. "The City Beautiful movement was fundamentally important to Kansas City," William Wilson writes in The City

Beautiful Movement in Kansas City. "It remade an ugly boomtown, giving it miles of graceful boulevards and parkways flanked by desirable residential sections, acres of ruggedly beautiful parkland dotted with recreational improvements, and several neighborhood playgrounds in crowded districts. Its results received attention and praise from city planners across the United States."

The City Beautiful movement began with the influence of one pastor. Twenty years later, in 1902, Hopkins left Kansas City to become the president of Williams College in Williamstown, Massachusetts. Heartbroken to lose its beloved pastor, the entire city honored Hopkins. A *Kansas City Star* article recognized the pastoral influence Hopkins held over the city, stating, "The position that the Rev. Henry Hopkins has occupied in this community has attracted notice because it has been almost unique. Few other ministers have had the confidence of those outside the church to a like degree." The *Star* also published a letter by W. H. Ramsay about Hopkins:

> It is not often that a minister holds such a place in the affections of the people generally as Dr. Hopkins holds in the hearts of the people of Kansas City. . . His success is a splendid testimonial to the power of consecrated manhood in the Christian ministry. Quietly, unostentatiously, without a shadow of sensationalism, Dr. Hopkins has done his splendid work, relying solely upon the power of Christian truth to make its own impression.

In a farewell banquet, one hundred prominent leaders of Kansas City gathered to honor the pastor. The speakers "all paid glowing tributes to Dr. Hopkins for what he was and for what he had done in and for Kansas City."

Swope Park and dozens of other parks and boulevards in the city came as the result of one man's sermon born out of a vision for the city. God used the city to foster creativity, and he used the church specially to spur that creativity to new heights.

Building a Convention Hall

As Kansas City grew, the city leaders didn't stop with parks. They decided to build a convention hall. After reconstruction from the Civil War, Kansas City was coming into its own as a bona fide city with a railroad and burgeoning downtown buildings. According to

Kansas City's first convention hall was constructed debt-free through citizens' donations.

The *Kansas City Spirit*, Kansas City had just come out of a building boom in the 1880s "followed by a bust that devastated the entire city and left it with a collection of ruffians, renegades, thieves, thugs, train robbers, prostitutes and all kinds of human wrecks. But out of the depths arose a citizenry of people filled with ambition, determination and energy."

The city leaders decided to build a convention center to show their growing unity and to mark themselves as a city. Noteworthy Christians such as August R. Meyer, Simeon B. Armour, and Kersey Coates were among the driving forces to get it built, rallying people together and donating their own money to see the hall constructed.

Upon the completion of the Convention Hall in 1899, the city leaders pulled together to bring in the famed evangelist Dwight L. Moody from Chicago. Moody had been preaching revivals nationwide over the previous forty years, and thousands had been

The interior of the Convention Hall. The evangelist D. L. Moody, one of the first speakers at the new hall, brought in a packed auditorium every night of his revival meetings.

DISCOVERING THE PAST TO SHAPE OUR FUTURE

coming to Christ. Hopkins and other Christian leaders in the city rallied for the great Chicago preacher to come host revival meetings in their brand-new hall. To finance Moody's coming, the church and the city worked together. Local businesses contributed to the cause, each pledging to finance a day of the revival. Moody did come and was the second to appear in the hall.

The fact that the city's leaders wanted to bring in Moody as soon as they had built the Convention Hall speaks of their values. They wanted to use the new trademark of the city to hold a revival. Kansas Citians were proud that their Convention Hall was built from citizens' donations, and they wanted Moody to know their story. The year after Moody passed away, his friend Rev. J. Wilbur Chapman wrote an account of Moody's life, *The Life and Work of Dwight Lyman Moody*. In the book, Chapman shares Moody's interactions with the press while visiting Kansas City:

> One of the reporters of the party said to him: "Do you know, Mr. Moody, how this building was put up? Do you know what it means to this city?"
>
> "No," said Mr. Moody, "I suppose some wealthy man owned it."
>
> "Kansas City owns it," was the answer. "Nearly every man and woman, hundreds of children contributed to its building, and own stock in it. It was built by gifts of the poor, as well as of the rich. It was built voluntarily by the people, and not by taxes. And it stands today as it stood the day it was finished, without a dollar of debt."
>
> At once Mr. Moody was intensely interested and demanded the story of the building. It was given him. "That is the sort of thing that annihilates anarchy," said Mr. Moody, in a burst of enthusiasm. "When I laid eyes on the hall, I said that there was no such hall in the country. But now that I know the sentiment and feeling that have been put into the hall, I know there is no other such building in the world. Do you know that when men are induced to unite as this city has united, where all classes of people behave as if they had common interests, a great lesson has been taught. The value of your hall, it strikes me, it is not in dollars and cents, but moral

significance. I did not believe that such a thing could be done in this generation. It has never been done before."

Moody praised Kansas City's unity, and Kansas City did not disappoint him. Crowds showed up in droves to listen to the evangelist, making the Kansas City revivals the largest audience Moody ever spoke in front of, as well as the largest gathering up to that date in the entire Mississippi Valley region. Thousands showed up for the first sermon. The Convention Hall held twenty-thousand people, yet they had to close and lock the doors because the hall quickly filled to capacity.

Even the Convention Hall's opening ceremonies did not attract such high numbers. Chapman wrote, "There had been notable gatherings in the great Convention Hall on former occasions, but even the dedication services, with the attraction of Sousa's Band and the appeal to civic pride, failed to bring together such a throng as that assembled to hear the man of God preach his plain, direct Gospel."

The first day of the revival, Moody preached a sermon on "Sowing and Reaping." He told his audience, "In after years, as you go by this building, I want you to remember this text that I am going to read to you. I pray that God will write it on every heart. It appeals to men and women of every sort and condition; to the priests and the ministers and the reporters: 'Be not deceived; God is not mocked: for whatsoever a man soweth, that shall he also reap. For he that soweth to his flesh shall of the flesh reap corruption; but he that soweth to the Spirit shall of the Spirit reap life everlasting.'"

> "[E]ven the dedication services . . . failed to bring together such a throng as that assembled to hear the man of God preach his plain, direct Gospel."

The last evening of the revivals, twenty thousand people crowded into the convention hall. Thousands more could not get in, so they opened Second Presbyterian Church across the street to hold the overflow crowds. That church quickly filled up as well, and they had to turn people away from both the Convention Hall and Second Presbyterian Church. The population of Kansas City at the

Dwight L. Moody's Last Sermon

Moody's Kansas City revival sermons proved to be his last. By Thursday evening, he was not doing well. His face was flushed; he was sweating profusely; and he took long pauses during his sermon, at times even stumbling from exhaustion. But he still preached a heartfelt message about the parable of the Great Supper in Luke 14, and he pleaded with the crowds to let go of their excuses and come to the Lord:

> "Now," said the preacher, "how many will accept this invitation? How many will say, 'I will?'" Then, as a number responded, the request was repeated. Still he lingered, his energies exhausted, and made one more appeal. "I'll wait a few minutes longer to see if anyone else, any man, woman or child, will say the word. I could stand here all night and listen to these 'I wills.'"

Moody would pass away a month later, and as Chapman observed, "He went away to his long rest with the sound of 'I will' spoken by those who were moved by his words still in his ears."

The next day, at noon on Friday, Moody decided he could not preach that afternoon as planned. After going out for a drive and returning to his armchair at the Coates' house, his face was puffy, his limbs were swelling, and "he had a feeling of oppression about his heart." He told his friends he would not be able to preach that day and asked Rev. Dr. Matt. S. Hughes, the pastor of the Independence Avenue Methodist Episcopal Church, to fill his spot, joking, "You Methodists are always prepared to preach." This was the first time Moody had to back out of a sermon, and he showed great regret at not being able to preach:

> "I'm afraid I shall have to give up the meetings," he said. "It's too bad." He was silent. "It's the first time in forty years of preaching that I have had to give up my meetings." He did not say anything for a while. Then he spoke in a low voice. "It is more painful to me to give up those audiences than it is to suffer from my ailments."

A physician visited Moody and pronounced that he needed to go home. As soon as possible that week, Moody boarded a train and headed back to Northfield, Massachusetts. Upon his return, he sent a telegraph to Kansas City, thanking "the good people of Kansas City for all their kindnesses."

Moody passed away the following month, three days before Christmas, surrounded by his family in his home in Massachusetts. Kansas City mourned along with the rest of the nation.

time was only 160,000, which means over a tenth of the city showed up for Moody's last revival sermon.

Robert A. Long, a lumber tycoon and dedicated member of Independence Boulevard Christian Church, led construction on Longview Farm, the Kansas City Museum, and the Liberty Memorial.

MVSC, KANSAS CITY PUBLIC LIBRARY

Then and Now

The Liberty Memorial has become a landmark in Kansas City. Towering on the hillside above Union Station, this solitary pillar has seen many eras go by. Its sweeping hillside has been leveled off into tiers, with stairways leading up to the memorial above and the fountain and American flag waving below. When the Royals won the World Series in 2015, masses of people packed the hillside. But that wasn't the first time celebrants crammed the space. Before that, one hundred thousand people had swarmed it in 1921 when Vice President Calvin Coolidge dedicated the site for the memorial. The Liberty Memorial was the brainchild of Robert A. Long.

Readers familiar with Lee's Summit, Missouri, will recognize the name "Long" from Longview Lake, Longview Farms Elementary, and Longview Community College—all named after Robert A. Long. Long impacted the Kansas City area in innumerable ways, from the Liberty Memorial to Longview Farm, to countless other elements of Kansas City.

The Liberty Memorial and Robert Long

To know Robert Long, we must go back to the 1800s before the Civil War, to a plantation in Kentucky. But this plantation operated differently. This plantation had no slaves. Its three hundred acres of farmland were owned by Robert Long's father, who lived out his deeply held convictions that slavery was wrong. This is the plantation where Robert Long spent his childhood. His father served as deacon in the Christian Church, and Long grew up with the high moral standards and religion of his family. Although the farm instilled a strong work ethic in Long, he didn't want to remain on the farm. His uncle had moved earlier to the newly formed state of Kansas, so Long left Kentucky to try to build a future in Columbus, Kansas. At the age of twenty-three, eight years after the Civil War, he ventured out into the Wild West.

Once Long arrived, his uncle helped him and another friend start a hay company. Unfortunately, the hay sales never took off, and they struggled to make ends meet. The company was failing, so they decided to scrap the business, literally. They tore down the barn that stored the hay and sold the lumber from the barn. It turned out that lumber was in high demand. The lumber sold so quickly, Long bought more lumber, which also sold right away. The lumber business went so well that he, his cousin Robert White, and another friend Victor Bell started a lumber company together. Soon his cousin passed away, so the remaining two—Bell and Long—bought out White's shares of the company and became the Long-Bell Lumber Company.

Their little company thrived. Along the way, Long met Ellie, a Pennsylvania Quaker who had moved out to Kansas to be a school teacher. They courted for a year and then married. Their first and only son died after living only a few weeks. They later had two little girls—Sallie America and Loula. The family moved to Kansas City just before the turn of the century and continued the lumber company there.

Immediately after moving to Kansas City, Long found a Disciples of Christ church to join. Long, Ellie, and his two daughters joined the Christian Church, which met in a small building located on the corner of Sixth and Prospect in Kansas City. As Long's career took off, he used his wealth to serve his church. In 1900 he bought property for the church to build a new building at the corners of Independence and Gladstone Boulevards. Five years later, when the building was completed, the congregation of approximately two hundred families moved into their new location and became Independence Boulevard Christian Church.

By 1909, the church's Sunday School class had grown quite large. According to the church's online history, Long challenged them that if they could have one thousand people in attendance for thirteen consecutive Sundays, he would build them an additional building. The church met the challenge, bumping up their attendance as high as sixteen hundred one Sunday, so Long added an educational building to the church, complete with "a gymnasium with running track and a swimming pool." Throughout his life, Long stayed dedicated to the church. Its church history states, "Until his death at the age of 84, Long attended church every Sunday and all church meetings."

Then and Now
The church continues today in Northeast Kansas City, running Micah Ministry, a ministry that partners with other local churches to serve the homeless.

After building the church, Long began constructing his own mansion. He bought out an entire city block in the same neighborhood as his church. He paid the few current homeowners well, and they relocated. They literally picked up their houses and moved them somewhere else. On that city block, Long built Corinthian Hall, reminiscent of the towering plantation homes of his childhood in Kentucky, with tall Corinthian pillars holding up the front porch, a veranda in the front, a large sweeping staircase in the entryway—the entryway where his second daughter Loula was married. The mansion had three levels, a carriage house behind the home, and other buildings scattered around the property. The library in the back of Corinthian Hall "was Long's private retreat, where he read the Bible each morning." The house overlooked the rolling hills of George Kessler Park and the scenic views of Cliff Drive.

Corinthian Hall, Long's home in Northeast Kansas City, now houses the Kansas City Museum.

DAVID ALAN SELBY

Then and Now
Long's mansion still stands today in Northeast Kansas City as the home of the Kansas City Museum.

After finishing Corinthian Hall, Long turned his attention toward construction on Longview Farm in Lee's Summit. Longview Farm was

> Corinthian Hall "was Long's private retreat, where he read the Bible each morning."

praised as the ideal dairy farm, having five major barn groups and forty-two different buildings. The name "Longview" says much about Long's perspective in life. He was always taking the long view, looking to the future, living out of wisdom for what would benefit the community and future generations. The Longs treated all their employees well, paying fair living wages and providing housing for all the staff. Whether he was building a farm or a lumberyard, he would always build housing for not just his staff, but for their families as well, so that the families could stay together while working for him.

At Longview Farm, all the staff lived on the property while they worked, and he built Longview Chapel, which still exists today, for them to attend church. Every year, Longview Chapel held a Christmas program for the farm's employees and families. After the program, Long's youngest daughter, Mrs. Loula Long Combs (married to Robert Pryor Combs), would hand out Christmas gifts for all the children. Donald Laney, whose father worked as a cowboy on Longview Farm in 1941, recalls his family's time on the farm: "My family felt very fortunate to live in such a beautiful place. . . . The Longs were kind, compassionate people who truly cared about their

Longview Farm (left) and Longview Mansion (above) in Lee's Summit, Missouri.

employees and their families. In my heart and the hearts of many, the Long family legacy will forever live on."

Long's lumber businesses were vertically integrated—he owned every aspect, from the first tree chopped down to the lumberyard that sold the tree. In that era, usually when men moved out to work in the lumber industry, they had to leave their families behind. They led a hard life, one that Long didn't want for his employees. He didn't want to separate his staff from their families, so he provided a way for their wives and children to live with them. In addition to providing housing for his employees and their families, he also provided for other aspects of their life. His sawmill city in Longview, Washington, had a library and a church for his workers. Whether a sawmill or a farm, Long built up his business endeavors as whole communities.

Long's influence stretched wide across Kansas City. He helped build churches, served as a trustee of the Bible College of Missouri, and joined multiple Christian organizations including the American Christian Mission Society, the National Brotherhood of Disciples of Christ, Christian Board of Publication, and the Men's and Millions Movement of the Christian Church. He also bought a publishing house that printed Christian literature.

However, what may perhaps be considered the crowning glory of Robert Long was Liberty Memorial. Just days after the United States signed the armistice ending World War I, Long sat at a dinner with twenty other business leaders in Kansas City. According to *Lest the Ages Forget*, "the conversation steered to a plan for construction of a 'Soldier Memorial.'" At the dinner, they tossed around different ideas of an art museum or other practical building for Kansas City, each idea costing four or five thousand dollars. *The Kansas City Times* records,

> [Then Long] rose and scorned the idea as far beneath the populace of a city such as Kansas City. "We should not erect a building for utilitarian purposes," he said. "Its constant use by future generations will in time desecrate it. We should construct for those veterans, who fought for liberty and the honor of our country, a monument that will reach into the skies and remain in everlasting tribute to their spirit of courage, honor, patriotism, and sacrifice."

Long proposed to them the idea of a giant memorial on the hillside across from Union Station—a multimillion-dollar project. As the city leaders listened, although they were intimidated by the cost, they knew it was the best idea. Long became head of the project to build Liberty Memorial. The city prepared for a fundraising campaign, and once it began, within two weeks the

A postcard advertises the dedication ceremony of the Liberty Memorial. Both President Calvin Coolidge and Queen Marie of Romania attended the ceremony in Kansas City.

Liberty Memorial Association had raised over $2.5 million to fund the project. Of course, Long donated $80,000 from his own fortune and from the Long-Bell Lumber Company.

Thousands crowded the hillside in 1921 for the groundbreaking ceremony and again five years later for the memorial's dedication. The dedication of 1926 brought in President Coolidge and even Queen Marie of Romania (the granddaughter of England's Queen Victoria) during her tour of the United States. The memorial includes Scripture references, and still today on the Liberty Memorial, you can read the Scriptures carved into it. The Historic American Buildings Survey describes the Scripture on the monument:

> Four inscriptions are carved above the figures of the frieze, two to a side. Above the figures of the three soldiers is the following: "Behold a pale horse and his / Name that sat on him was death / And Hell followed with him" [Revelation 6:8]. The inscription above the figures of the nurse and wounded men reads: "Violence shall no more be heard / In thy land wasting nor / Destruction within thy borders" [Isaiah 60:18]. To the west of the central figure, above the two groups (moving east to west) reads the following: "What doth the LORD require of thee / But to do justly and to love mercy / And to walk humbly with thy God" [Micah 6:8]. The final passage evokes a message of assurance: "Then shall the earth yield / Her increase and God / Even our own God shall bless us" [Psalm 67:6].

The Christian faith is embedded into the very stone of one of the most iconic landmarks in Kansas City, thanks to Long and his influence over the city.

Beyond Church Walls

Throughout Kansas City's history, Christians like Long have recognized that their role in the kingdom of God reaches far beyond the four walls of a church building. Mrs. Cox trudged through mud paths from house to house, starting neighborhood Bible studies and prayer meetings. Reverend Hopkins looked beyond the city's dirt roads and saw the beauty it could become. He preached about embodying Christ in every occupation every day of the week, and he lived out his sermons in daily life, gaining the respect and affection of an entire city. His worldview spread to others in his congregation, and the city reaped the benefits as parks and boulevards sprang up.

Christian leaders Armour, Coates, and Meyer led the way in bringing a Convention Hall to Kansas City. Within the first year the hall was completed, they brought in a nationally renowned evangelist to hold a citywide revival. Long also allowed his faith to infiltrate every aspect of life. He took care of his employees and built housing for them. He took care of his church and built a new sanctuary when they expanded. He took care of the environment by being the first lumber company to replant the forests it cut down. And he cared for the city, leading the way in building a monument covered in Scripture that stands today near the heart of Kansas City.

These Christians saw no separation between church life and civic life. Jesus views the church the same way. In Matthew 5, He tells us, "You are the salt of the earth," and "You are the light of the world." The church is meant to preserve the city and bring new life. Throughout our history, Kansas City's Christians have done just that. We can thank their service for so much of the beauty we enjoy in our city today. The leaders named in this chapter are just a few of the thousands of Christians who have helped shape the city. From the City Beautiful movement to Liberty Memorial, Christians' influence has formed more than buildings; it has impacted millions of lives and left a permanent imprint on Kansas City.

Chapter 6
Mobsters and Madams
...
(1900 – 1939)

Walking up to the towering stone front of Union Station, if you look to the left of the golden-brass doors at the eastern entrance, you can see a small, bullet-sized indent about seven feet up on the granite wall. The hole allegedly came from a shooting in 1933, referred to as the "massacre at Union Station." On June 17, four law enforcement officers were transporting an escaped convict, Frank Nash, back to prison in Leavenworth, Kansas. They arrived by train that morning at Union Station. As the officers were loading Nash into a Chevrolet to drive him to Leavenworth, an unknown gunman yelled, "Let 'em have it!" Immediately, three gunmen started firing machine guns at the officers. In a moment, all four officers and Nash lay dead. When the gunmen realized Nash was dead, they fled the scene by car.

The suspected gunmen—Vernon Miller, Adam Richetti, and Charles "Pretty Boy" Floyd—were found guilty of the crime. Both Miller and Floyd were murdered in other incidents before they were apprehended for the Union Station Massacre. The third suspect, Richetti, was tried in court, convicted, and sentenced to death. Although historians later debated who had actually committed the shooting, the shooting reflects an era of crime. During the 1920s and into the 1930s, the mob ruled Kansas City. According to historian Jason Roe, the escalating violence "gave the city a reputation for organized crime that, at least for a time, was second only to Chicago." In a classic fight for good and evil, the church found itself in the thick of the fray.

The Machine Begins

The Roaring 1920s was an age of contradiction. Across the United States, American citizens fought for social reforms such as prohibition and votes for women. It was a country trying to right its moral wrongs. At the same time, speakeasies popped up, and noteworthy criminals such as Al Capone or Bonnie and Clyde surfaced. Many American cities fell under the power of political bosses and machine organizations, and Kansas City was no exception. Remember, the river always seemed to bring the good and the bad.

The cogs of Kansas City's mob machine started turning back in 1876, when Jim Pendergast moved to Kansas City to work in a West Bottoms factory. Jim was a Pendergast, but he was not *the* Pendergast—for those of you familiar with Tom Pendergast, the mob boss who ruled Kansas City for decades. The Pendergast machine first began with Tom's older brother, Jim.

Jim started out as a regular Irish worker in the West Bottoms. He placed a bet on a racetrack horse, won, and used his prize money to buy a saloon. Through the saloon, he did much more than serve drinks to his customers. He ran an unofficial bank within the saloon, loaning money to the poor in the West Bottoms. He counseled and befriended the working class, and through favors he won the hearts of West Bottoms' poor and immigrants because he was one of them. In 1892, residents of the West Bottoms elected Jim as their alderman.

During his nineteen years as alderman, Jim "consistently got what he wanted for his district," according to *Journeys Through Time*. Before passing away in 1911, Jim recommended his younger brother Tom as his successor. So Tom Pendergast was elected. Tom continued his brother's political control as alderman but soon realized he could have more control over the city through business than politics, and he stepped down after five years as alderman.

Over the next two decades, Tom Pendergast ("Pendergast") gained control of the state Democratic Party through "fraud, manipulation, and violence at the ballot box as well as service to the people of Kansas City and Jackson County," according to the State Historical Society of Missouri. He manipulated politics and elections, and he maintained rule through the underworld of organized crime. At the same time, like his brother, he made sure to always give favors to the poor.

Mob boss Tom Pendergast unofficially ruled Kansas City through machine politics from the early 20th century through the Great Depression.

History is rarely black and white regarding which side is right and which side is wrong. The Pendergast machine gained power through corruption, but it did much good for the city. The jazz age thrived under Pendergast's rule. The saloons incorporated jazz in their entertainment and made Kansas City famous as a jazz city.

Moreover, Pendergast stayed in power because he cared for people. He watched out for the little man, the underdog in society. Like his brother Jim, he befriended the poor and the immigrants. He knew what the people needed, and he knew how to help them.

Especially during the Great Depression, as people were hungry, desperate for jobs, and fearful of the future, Pendergast provided hope. If someone was impoverished, the machine would provide Christmas presents for their children. If someone was unemployed, the machine would find them a job and make sure they kept it. If someone was new to town and didn't know anyone, after the first or second day in their new home, they would get a knock on the door. The visitor would say, "Hi, I'm from the Democratic Party. Here's who you can call to get your gas turned on. Here's a bundle of logs, and I put a bag of coal in your shed. Call us if you ever need anything else."

On the other hand, although the machine did good for the city, it was run through corruption. Machine leaders rigged the voting system to stay in power. Come voting day, the machine would hire people to vote under the names of dead people. Machine-hired voters would travel from poll to poll across the county, even "riding Machine-chartered busses to the most remote precincts in Jackson County" to cast their votes. One year at the polls, four people were murdered. Corruption ran rampant.

Pendergast was an Irish Catholic, and the Catholic Church worked closely with the machine. Zach Daughtrey, the historian for the Kansas City Diocese, shared that by no means would the Catholic church have approved of the vices that Pendergast endorsed.

"The Church would have abhorred the vice that went on with the machine," Daughtrey said. But the machine got things done. The machine cared for the poor and for immigrants, two priorities of the Catholic Church. According to Daughtrey, "The Catholic Church understood that Pendergast, the machine, and the Democratic Party were a major part of running Kansas City. So they tried to work in a positive way to assist the people."

Resisting Legalized Vice

Under Pendergast's rule, crime flourished. The Missouri governor had previously placed a ban on saloons in residential areas. However, that ban expired the same year Pendergast was

> "They tried to work in a positive way to assist the people."

elected. Also that year, new police commissioners were appointed in Kansas City—ones who had much more lenient stances on saloons. The new police issued licenses to twenty-six saloons in residential areas of Kansas City. Moreover, they discharged those police who had supported keeping saloons out of neighborhoods, and they hired corrupt new policemen "who are notoriously identified with the most vicious elements of society," according to a complaint letter from the Good Government League.

With the new policemen in power, corruption thrived—brothels, gambling, and alcohol. Instead of eradicating illegal activity, the police simply charged fines: They charged thirty dollars per month to a brothel and an extra twenty dollars if the brothel served alcohol. This system kept corruption in business and also ensured that the city profited from corruption. The city kept these vice businesses confined to the red-light district on the north end.

At the same time Pendergast came to power, the United States was entering the prohibition era, where religious moralists from the Victorian era took a strong stance against alcohol and other vices, and alcohol was outlawed nationwide. Values clashed as the moralists were gaining ground, fighting for reform across the United States, but the mob stayed in charge of the city. Instead of serving as a place of refuge, the city now served as a hotbed for crooks.

As churches saw corruption overtaking the city, they rose up to resist. Churches in the city started a campaign to try to clean up the vice district. The churches accused the city of letting crime increase because of its lenient stances, and they campaigned the city to shut down the vice district, especially the brothels. Taking a stand against vice, churches banded together and formed the Church Federation of Kansas City. In 1913, the Church Federation reorganized as the Society for the Suppression of Commercialized Vice and successfully convinced the city to close the red-light district. They stated their purpose as wanting to stop the "deathly march of human lechery and moral degeneracy in our midst."

Their organization was inspired by the death of an eighteen-year-old Westport high school girl, Met Zook, who passed away in the spring of that year, presumably from activities related to prostitution. Their statement begins, "The Society for Suppression of Commercialized Vice was organized in October 1913. The moral sense of Kansas City had been shocked by the tragic death of a high school girl, and the public demanded that the houses of prostitution should be banished from the city." Their statement continues, "Meetings were held nearly every day. The co-operation of the police, the prosecuting attorney, and the courts was secured. . . Within one week from the organization of the Society there was not an open house of prostitution in Kansas City."

In a series of night raids, the police commissioners evicted four hundred women from the brothels. After the evictions, prostitution spread throughout the city. In the weeks following the raids, reports sprang up that "streetwalkers were operating in formerly chaste residential neighborhoods." While the churches had good intentions of purifying the city, their efforts only served to spread crime, not eradicate it.

> While the churches had good intentions of purifying the city, their efforts only served to spread crime, not eradicate it.

For the next ten years, as the Pendergast machine grew in power, the Society worked to rid Kansas City of vice. In 1923, they listed on their ten-year report that they were receiving help from "the Federation of Men's Bible Classes." The men's Bible classes led by Napoleon W. Dible were a phenomenon the year before, in 1922, that brought together nearly every church in the city.

Architect Napoleon W. Dible led the world's largest men's Bible study through First Baptist Church of Kansas City.

DAVID ALAN SELBY

Then and Now

The name Dible might not sound familiar, but as you drive down Ward Parkway, you've likely seen his Tudor-style houses lining the road with their steeply sloped roofs, arched doorways, and circular towers. In the winter, covered in snow and Christmas lights, they glow like gingerbread houses cut straight out of a fairytale book.

DISCOVERING THE PAST TO SHAPE OUR FUTURE

KANSAS CITY LEGACY
...
William Volker
"THE RIGHTEOUS WILL BE REMEMBERED FOREVER..." PSALM 112:6

Volker Boulevard runs south of the Nelson Atkins Museum of Art.

One member of the board of directors for the Society for Suppression of Commercialized Vice was William Volker. Most Kansas Citians recognize the name from Volker Boulevard, which runs parallel to Brush Creek, just south of the Nelson-Atkins Museum of Art.

A generous philanthropist, William Volker earned the title, "Mr. Anonymous," because he always asked that his gifts remain anonymous. Volker gave millions toward large projects such as building the University of Kansas City (now UMKC). He supported education, hospitals, and construction in Kansas City. However, no cause was too small for him. When a boy's bicycle was stolen at a school, Volker bought the boy a replacement. When a family couldn't afford a graduation dress for their daughter, Volker stepped in and bought the dress.

Every day, an average of fifty to sixty people visited Volker's office seeking financial aid. Black or white, rich or poor, Jew, Protestant or Catholic—Volker helped anyone who was in need. Volker also served on the board of directors for the Society for Suppression of Commercialized Vice, fighting the rampant spread of corruption during the Pendergast era.

William Volker was an earnest and habitual reader of the Scriptures. When describing Volker, his nephew Harold Luhnow said, "He never lost his childlike faith in what he called providence."

When dedicating the William Volker Memorial Fountain, *Kansas City Star* reporter Henry Haskell said of Volker, "His sympathy responded to every form of distress. His practical vision matched his generosity. And his modesty enveloped all three."

William Volker left a legacy of generosity toward all in need.

The World's Largest Business Men's Bible Class

The unique sloped-roof, Tudor-style houses were a trademark of Dible's designs in the 1920s. Dible was well known in Kansas City as an architect, and his houses still fill Ward Parkway and the Brookside and Waldo areas. He had four basic floor plans, and his goal was to build affordable, well-built homes. His company made their profit by selling homes at a low price but selling lots of them. Dible kept a tight rein on the business: "He called his salesmen after dinner each night for a daily report, asking each one, 'What's it going to be, steak or hot dogs?'" writes historian Susan Jezak Ford.

Dible was hardworking and disciplined. Ford writes, "Dible followed a rigorous schedule in his business and personal life. He never took a day off work, ate his meals at the same time every day, and did one hundred push-ups a day into his 80s." His hard work paid off. His company built over five thousand homes in Kansas City, leaving his trademark housing style in many neighborhoods. Over a fifty-year period, Dible's company planned out and built thousands of homes both in Kansas City and in the suburbs.

He took pride in making them built to last. A hundred years later, his houses are still in demand for their high quality that has endured through time.

Dible carried this same dedication and ambition from his housing business into his service at his church. In the 1920s, it was popular for churches to have a businessmen's Bible study, and Dible's church was no exception. When the president of William Jewell College, Dr. David Jones Evans, stepped down from his presidency to pastor First Baptist Church of Kansas City, he recruited Dible to lead the church's Business Men's Bible Class. Starting at just thirty-five members, Dible brought the class membership into the thousands. Once the class hit twenty-five hundred people per week, it became so large that the church built a separate wing that was bigger than their sanctuary just to accommodate the Bible study.

In 1922, the study had a surge of members, bringing their numbers to thirty-seven hundred. Excited about how many men were showing up for the Bible study, Dible researched to see if there were any business men's Bible studies bigger than theirs. He found one group larger in Long Beach, California. In a friendly, competitive spirit, he wrote the Long Beach Bible study a letter saying Kansas City would take away their title the next year. Dible organized the study into a military model, with captains and lieutenants over groups of fifty and one hundred. He rallied men together to become

Business men fill the streets of downtown Kansas City for a Sunday morning rally of the World's Largest Men's Bible Class.

the largest Bible study. One Sunday morning in 1923, men in suits flooded the streets of Kansas City with a banner over their heads that read, "World's Largest Business Men's Bible Class, 52,121 men." On the day of the event, seventy-five buglers rode through the city, sounding the call. The mayor of Independence came, as well as Missouri Governor Arthur Hyde.

At the time of the rally, the city's entire population was 324,000 people. This means that over 15 percent of the city showed up for the rally. The rally was on a Sunday morning, and presumably the majority of churches in town participated. At the time of the rally, the Pendergast machine was in full gear. Down the street were Tom Pendergast's racetracks and the saloons that openly flaunted breaking the prohibition laws. Yet a large chunk of the city's men showed up for the Bible study. After this one-time rally, the study returned to its regular attendance of twenty-five hundred to three thousand people. It continued for approximately the next ten years, into 1930. As the Society for Suppression of Commercialized Vice indicated in their report, after the rally, the men's Bible classes continued to play an active role in fighting corruption throughout the city.

A Life Changed Through Love

The Society received the strongest resistance from Annie Chambers, owner of the largest and longest-standing brothel in town, the Chambers Mansion. The Society's ten-year report included a special section titled, "The Annie Chambers Case." In the report, they complained, "Through political influence and the leniency of the courts she managed to 'get by' when other places had been closed."

WORLD'S LARGEST MEN'S BIBLE CLASS
52,121 MEN   KANSAS CITY, MO.
SUNDAY NOV. 11, 1923

FIRST BAPTIST CHURCH OF KANSAS CITY

Seemingly indomitable, Chambers refused to back down when other brothels closed. Chambers's story began before the Civil War. We tend to split history into different periods—the Civil War, Reconstruction, Prohibition, etc. Yet each person lives through several periods. We must remember that the stories are all connected and influence each era. At the beginning of the Civil War, Chambers was a teenager. Her family moved from Kentucky to Indiana. Although they moved north, her father kept his Confederate sympathies.

A parade came through their town in support of President Lincoln. At seventeen years old, Chambers wanted to go out with her friends and have fun. She didn't care about the political views. So she rode a horse in the parade. Unfortunately, her father saw her riding in the parade. Enraged, he kicked her out of the house, sending her to live with her aunt.

Needing to support herself financially, she became a schoolteacher. A few years later, she met a man, fell in love, and married him. Unfortunately,

Annie Chambers ran the largest brothel in town until her dramatic conversion after City Union Mission's pastor moved in next door.

MVSC, KANSAS CITY PUBLIC LIBRARY

DISCOVERING THE PAST TO SHAPE OUR FUTURE

the tragedies continued. She and her husband lost their first child. Then during her second pregnancy, she was riding in a buggy when a bird flew out of a bush and spooked the horse. Chambers was thrown from the buggy, and the spill sent her into a coma for three days. When she awoke, she found out her second baby was stillborn. To add to her grief, she found out that two more tragedies had occurred during those three days: Her husband had fallen from a railroad trestle and died, and her father had lost a hotel he had purchased, leaving the family bankrupt.

Chambers now faced life as a grieving widow and bereft mother disowned by her bankrupt family. Back in those days, to be a schoolteacher you had to be "certifiably virginal," which she was not. Her friend worked in a millinery in Indianapolis, making hats, so Chambers went to Indianapolis. But the working conditions at the millinery were terrible. The women stayed in a room and worked twenty hours per day, ate nothing but oatmeal, and earned four dollars a week—a small sum even in the nineteenth century. Chambers went to join her friend but did not want the harsh conditions of the millinery.

Then a lady from a "resort" in Indianapolis came to the millinery to recruit women. She said, "If you ever get tired of working so hard for so little, come see me."

> **"If you ever get tired of working so hard for so little, come see me."**

Chambers realized she could make good money from prostitution. She arrived at the resort (brothel) numb from grief, and she determined she was "going to have a short life, but a fast and merry one." She went into prostitution for years. To add to the tragedy, she fell in love with one of her clients and was planning on marrying him when she found out he already had a wife. Devastated, she decided to leave Indianapolis and venture to Kansas City. Back then, it was still the boisterous cow town, and she heard business was good in the city. She rented a little cabin and soon upgraded, building a twenty-four-room mansion in the red-light district south of the river (what is now the City Market area). By this time, she was older and made money by employing other girls in prostitution at the mansion. She advertised by sending decorative invitations to all the men of the city at their work addresses.

When the Church Federation banded together as the Society for Suppression of Commercialized Vice to shut down all the brothels in the city, Chambers argued that shutting them down wouldn't change the existence of prostitution in the city. It would simply get rid of having a centralized place for the women to do business and would thus spread prostitution throughout the city's neighborhoods.

The Society didn't listen to her. They campaigned and convinced the city to shut down the brothels. The police conducted the night raids, and after the evictions, Chambers's warning proved true: Prostitution spread throughout the city.

The laws didn't change anything. Moreover, Chambers didn't agree with the new law, so she took her case to the Supreme Court of Missouri. The court ruled in her favor, stating, "Keeping a bawdy house . . . is not a public nuisance in any sense of the term." She won the case, but by this time, she was seventy-nine years old. She had lived a long, hard life and was beginning to give up on her struggle to keep her mansion open. Around the same time, she also met David and Beulah Bulkley.

Rev. David Bulkley and his wife, Beulah, founded the homeless shelter City Union Mission.

Then and Now

Perhaps you've heard of City Union Mission, which continues today as the largest and oldest homeless shelter in Kansas City. It has run continuously since it was opened in 1924 by Rev. David Bulkley.

Rev. Bulkley moved into the vice district with his wife, Beulah, and their daughter. They opened a homeless shelter there, City Union Mission. Most of the brothels had shut down with the city's reforms, leaving behind vacant buildings with lots of rooms—perfect for a homeless shelter. Bulkley bought the Lovejoy Mansion, a former brothel which happened to stand next door to Chambers's mansion.

So here was a pastor, his wife and daughter, staying in Madame Lovejoy's old suite. An article in the *Kansas City Star* reported on the Bulkleys' mission, "In the room of Madame Lovejoy, on the first floor, with the trap door in the corner through which she used to draw up the wine and other liquors from the iced troughs in the cellar, Dave and his wife and daughter set up housekeeping." The Bulkleys ran the homeless shelter; Chambers ran her boarding house. Though next door to each other, the households could not have been farther apart in their beliefs.

By this point, Chambers was eighty-one and had hip problems, so she sat in her living room most of each day. Her living room window opened up to the City Union Mission, and as she sat in her house one day, she heard Rev. Bulkley preaching a sermon. She listened in. He was preaching a funeral sermon for a woman who had just lost her baby. Although it had been decades since Chambers had lost her own children, her grief was still fresh. As she listened, the sermon took her back to when she had lost her children. She was moved.

Years later, an alcohol distiller at a brewery in their neighborhood caught on fire. The fire department came to contain the fire, and all the neighbors came out on the street, first to see what was going on, and then to watch as the distillery burned. Chambers stood next to the Bulkleys, and as they watched the fire, she asked Beulah Bulkley if they could be friends. Chambers later told the *Kansas City Star* the contents of her conversation with Beulah:

> I know what you have been doing. I have been watching you. I heard the sermon your husband

Bulkley stands outside of City Union Mission, located in the heart of Kansas City's "vice district."

preached over that woman's baby. I know about that Scotchman, for years the most notorious drunkard of the North End, that you took into your own home and reformed. I know about the man who was dying in prison but did not want to die there, so you got him out and brought him to your home here that he might die out of prison. I've been watching you. I want you to be my friends.

From that night on, they were friends. They became good friends, in fact, and through their relationship, Chambers decided to follow Christ. The Bulkleys looked after her in her old age—bringing her meals, reading the Bible to her, and praying with her. She became a Christian and spent the remainder of her life speaking out about the evils of sin. Upon her death in 1935, she bequeathed her boarding house to City Union Mission. Before passing away, she said,

> Isn't it strange that in this house where so many women have led a life so far from what was right, now I, the worst of them all, have turned the place into a mission for the saving of just such women and am preaching to them the gospel of salvation? That old book, the Bible, is a great comfort to me, but of all its beautiful texts the best, to me, is the promise: "Though your sins be as scarlet, they shall be white as snow, though they be red like crimson, they shall be as wool."

The story of Annie Chambers illustrates how God can change any life. Even the ringleader of corruption can come to Christ. The Society focused on changing the law, but the Bulkleys focused on renewing the heart through God's love.

Dismantling the Machine

By the time the Bulkleys moved next door to Annie Chambers, the Pendergast machine was in full gear. As brothels shut down in Kansas City, citizens turned their attention toward speaking out against the corruption of the machine.

Rabbi Samuel Mayerberg of Temple B'nai Jehudah was the first public city leader to speak out against the machine.

Mayerberg was described as having "a wiry, energetic presence before the congregation, combining passionate speech with a scholar's eloquence." He advocated from his pulpit that it was the minister's duty to speak out against evil. He said, "[W]here iniquity runs rampant, where depraved and selfish men prey upon the community, it is not only the right but also the responsibility of the minister to lead in the movement to eradicate such evil powers."

> "It is the responsibility of the minister to lead in the movement to eradicate such evil powers."
>
> -Rabbi Samuel Mayerberg

His first place to publicly expose the Pendergast machine was in 1932 at a local women's group meeting, the Government Study Club. He did not mince his words but told them plainly, "You've turned your city over to a gang and given it into the hands of crooks and racketeers because you've been asleep." A cub reporter attended the meeting and published Mayerberg's comments in the *Kansas City Star* that evening beneath the headline "Crooks Run the City." From that point on, Mayerberg had a target on his back, as far as the machine was concerned. The fight was on.

Mayerberg pulled together ministers from all faiths, civic organizations, and clubs, and he led the Ministerial Alliance in working to recall the entire city council. He received public support from many citizens, and they even encouraged him to run for mayor.

However, to speak out against the machine held great risk, since Pendergast ruled through intimidation. Mayerberg received death threats. The governor of Missouri assigned bodyguards to protect the rabbi. Mayerberg slept with a pistol under his pillow, just in case. He installed bulletproof windows in his car, and thankfully so, since later he was shot at while driving. The violence against him became so concerning that he had to leave Kansas City and relocate to another city for a time.

Fred Olander Sr. was another Kansas City citizen who spoke out against the machine. He had always wanted to be a pastor but ended up working in the stockyards in the West Bottoms, as president of the Kansas City Livestock Exchange. However, he still had a heart for righteousness. Olander, Mayerberg and others put together the clean sweep to try to dismantle the machine. Grassroots civic efforts were what started turning the city around. The citizens went up against the machine, not knowing who would win.

By the late 1930s, the clean sweep efforts won out. Over two hundred fifty machine workers were convicted of various charges of election fraud. Eventually, in 1939 Pendergast himself was convicted of income tax evasion, and he was sentenced to fifteen months in federal prison. Not for murder. Not for corrupting the polls. Just for income tax evasion. Thus ended over four decades of the Pendergast era.

Both Law and Grace

During Kansas City's Pendergast years, churches responded to the machine in three different ways. Some joined the machine in order to effectively serve the poor. Others fought vice through legal reform. Still others chose to share Christ on a personal level.

Can we say one response was right and the others were wrong? Or that one way was effective, and the others were ineffective? Each group had a different goal and responded to the crisis to meet their goals however they thought best. To the Catholic churches, it seemed that the mob was there to stay, so they made the most of a difficult time and worked with the machine and the Democratic Party to serve the poor and the immigrants. The Church Federation decided that laws and legal reform were the best way to fight corruption, and they threw their energy into shutting down the vice district. Although they succeeded, vice still continued across the city in different forms. And finally, the Bulkleys chose to move into the vice district and personally care for the homeless, addicts, and exploited women instead of condemning them. They lived out the gospel of grace and saw peoples' hearts turn to Jesus through their ministry. The Pendergast era left Kansas City's churches with much to process.

Although churches gave their attention to fighting the vices of gambling, prostitution, and political corruption, they paid little attention to the evil of racism. The decades ahead would force churches to confront this issue as well.

Chapter 7
Seeds of Change
(1910 - 1965)

Just blocks away from Eighteenth and Vine, Kansas City's historic Jazz District, stands an equally historic building—the headquarters of *The Call*, Kansas City's one-hundred-year-old African American newspaper. The paper was founded in 1919 out of a need for the black community to have a voice concerning the issues they faced. During the 1920s to1950s, in the years following the Pendergast era, the issue of segregation rose to the forefront of public consciousness, both across the nation and in Kansas City. While some church members fought to maintain segregation, others went to great efforts to see reconciliation. As racial tension and hostility increased, these churches' efforts for peace would prepare Kansas City for the civil rights movement.

Housing Segregation Takes Root

After the Civil War, because of limited educational and career opportunities, African American families found themselves in poverty even forty years after the Civil War had ended. A large portion of black families had come to Kansas City as Exodusters with few belongings. Many of them found jobs in the railroad and meatpacking industries and acclimated into Kansas City's community. In the decades following the Exoduster migration, black families continued to pour into the city looking for jobs, for better education for their children, and for an escape from the animosity of the South. Up through 1900, although racial divisions existed, there had been no official housing segregation in Kansas City. However, as the black community grew, white residents felt threatened by their presence. From 1900 to 1920, the city's black population grew by 70 percent. As it grew, white communities started taking action to ensure that their neighborhoods remained segregated. They fought the encroachment of black families in white neighborhoods.

Many black workers were limited to unskilled labor positions and lived in low-income areas. In addition to their limited financial opportunities, they faced discrimination from the police. Police did not enforce the law adequately in black neighborhoods, so crime ran rampant. Moreover, the city relegated its "vice" businesses to the north end of the city where the black neighborhoods were. Because of lack of law enforcement and a flood of vice businesses, white communities began to associate "black" with poverty, violence, and crime, and insisted on keeping black families out of their neighborhoods.

Black neighborhoods became overcrowded, but when they tried to move out between 1910 and 1920, "whites tried to repel them with dynamite, statutes, and covenants," according to historian Sherry Lamb Schirmer's book *A City Divided: The Racial Landscape of Kansas City, 1900–1960*. This discrimination was most evident in the Vine Street corridor (today the Eighteenth and Vine District, east of MLK Jr Blvd). With nowhere else for families to go, the corridor kept filling up. Because of the cramped, inadequate housing, the mortality rate for black people was twice that of white people in 1912. Disease ran rampant, due to "inadequate diet, hard labor, and poor living conditions."

Kansas City had the first municipal welfare agency in the nation: the Bureau of Public Welfare. It released two reports in 1912 and 1913—one on housing and one on social well-being. Both reports blamed black residents for poverty and urban squalor, saying black citizens were "steeped in crime, with lost virtue, and without purpose and without hope." At the same time a local civics teacher, Asa Martin, published a master's thesis titled *Our Negro Population*. His report "equated black Kansas Citians with disorderly conduct and criminality, unclean habits, immorality, and the deterioration of property." These reports equated environment with character. They also scared white families from sharing neighborhoods with black neighbors.

With the segregation, black citizens formed their own communities, including their own churches. Between 1900 and 1915, more than a dozen churches sprang up along the North End's Vine Street corridor. Another North End black community, called Church Hill, formed around Allen Chapel A.M.E. and Second Baptist, the city's two oldest black congregations. The churches drew in families by offering community centers, events, and recreation, as well as places of worship. Black communities may have been more involved in church life than their white counterparts. In 1927 historian Olive Hoggins recorded 367 churches in Kansas City and noted that eighty of them were black congregations. While black residents comprised 10 percent of the city's total population, they accounted for 20 percent of the city's churches.

The Church Responds

As social tension grew, the white church could no longer ignore racial animosity. In 1910 a group of churchmen met at St. George's

Episcopal Church to debate "the Negro problem," and "whites who might be goaded into lawlessness in reaction to black crime." The churchmen discussed the issue, but nothing came from this meeting except a reinforcement of their fear of black people living in their neighborhoods.

Indeed, the church group's worry of violence from whites was well-founded. In 1910 and 1911, six black families were bombed after moving into white neighborhoods on the outer edge of the black eastside in northern Kansas City. Through the next half decade, "white flight" occurred as whites fled their neighborhoods once black neighbors moved in. Many black citizens felt trapped since the black residential areas of the city were overpopulated, but they were prohibited from moving to other areas within the city.

There was a double standard among Christians. In 1915, J. C. Nichols, when designing the Country Club District, "appointed a committee of six to seven men representing as many of the larger denominations to look over all the undeveloped Country Club territory to select sites for churches." Although Nichols was careful to include the churches in designing his neighborhoods, he was also careful to exclude other groups, writing clauses in the housing deeds that prohibited homeowners from selling or renting to black buyers. In the book *A City Divided*, Schirmer shares a detailed account of segregation in Kansas City. When the faculty of Western College, a Bible school for black students, wanted to relocate to a vacant mansion in a white neighborhood, white residents protested the Bible college. They convinced the city council to pass a law in 1915 forbidding schools for students "of African descent" to be within twenty-four hundred feet of a school for whites. Nelson C. Crews, a prominent black politician and owner of *The Kansas City Sun*, observed, "So-called refined, fair, [C]hristian people have met and solemnly vowed that the school must not come near them and that they will keep it away at any cost . . ."

> "So-called refined, fair, [C]hristian people have met and solemnly vowed that the school must not come near them . . ."
>
> -Nelson C. Crews

Though some churchgoers fought to maintain segregation, others worked for racial equality. In 1919 the mayor of Kansas City formed a committee of prominent black and white Kansas Citians to protect black residents. The committee included five white men and six black men. Several of them were noteworthy Christians, including Robert A. Long, lumber manufacturer; Rev. Burris Jenkins, clergyman and editor of the *Post*; Rev. William H. Thomas, pastor of Allen Chapel A.M.E. Church; and Charles W. Armour, whose family started the Armour Home and Orphan's Home, and whose aunt, Margaret Armour, served as president of the Women's Christian Association, and whose uncle distributed food to the Exodusters when they first arrived. This group proved that different races could work together harmoniously. They searched for areas of the community where black families could buy housing. Schirmer records in *A City Divided*,

> [C]ommittee members acted swiftly to calm fears and squelch inflammatory rumors among both races. Although the committee's plans to designate a safe area for black residential expansion never materialized, its preemptive rumor-control measures, along with modest in-migration by black southerners, may have had some effect. While race riots tormented Chicago and Omaha that summer, Kansas City escaped the terrors of mob violence.

In addition to the mayor's group, the Citizen's League formed a committee of their own, the Inter-Racial Committee, consisting of twelve Kansas City residents—six black and six white. This group included two pastors of large congregations. While many Christians turned a blind eye to racial matters, others endeavored to bring reconciliation to a divided city.

These committees delegated to keeping the peace proved necessary as segregation continued. During the 1920s, as the city grew, efforts to keep it segregated continued. Realtors noticed that once black families moved into a neighborhood, the property value would decline, so realtors formed the Southeast Home Protective Association. According to *A City Divided*, "The organization's prime purpose, according to its handbill, was to prevent 'the encroachment of Negroes' by shunning property owners, real estate agents, and lenders who enabled African Americans to move into the area." They encouraged homeowners to enter into covenants that ensured they would only sell their homes to white residents. *A City Divided* tells story after story of bombings on black residents' houses whenever they moved into an all-white neighborhood. In 1923, a bomb went off in a neighborhood they were trying to protect, damaging every house on the block, in an effort to scare black families from moving in.

Churches were divided on the issue of segregation. Some churches supported housing covenants and segregation, while other churches worked together to find peace. Churches fell on both sides, just as the city itself did. Some white churches jumped on board with supporting segregation. The Linwood Improvement Association (LIA) tried to maintain an all-white housing district south of the black district, and they found support from churches in the area. Developers often used parks at the edge of a housing area to control what was next to it and to protect new housing areas from "undesirable land use." In the Linwood area, between Twenty-Seventh and Thirty-First Streets, where US Highway 71 now cuts through, the Linwood Improvement Association tried to protect their homes from black families moving into the neighborhood by bordering the neighborhood with a park on the north side, separating them from the designated black housing in the city. Realtor John Bowman, president of the association, gained the support of local churches in his fight for segregation. For a year, the LIA petitioned the city to approve the park, but the city kept refusing. LIA sent letters of threat to realtors and black homeowners. *The Call* received a letter from LIA saying, "We want those sixty-two negro homes for a park, and we are going to have them if we are compelled to blow every one of them up."

Planting Seeds of Reconciliation

Amid the violence of divided churches, one group in particular worked together, laying groundwork that would pave the way for the civil rights movement twenty years later. A Christian pacifist movement, the Fellowship of Reconciliation, played an instrumental role in preparing the way for peaceful racial reconciliation in Kansas City. The Fellowship of Reconciliation (FOR) was founded in America in 1915, just one year after World War I began. FOR was established by Christian pacifists who worked for "world order based on love." By 1930 a branch of the organization had grown in Kansas City. They began as an anti-war organization in the midst of World War I and continued their peace efforts up through the beginning of

World War II. As the second World War broke out, the Kansas City chapter of FOR was disheartened that their efforts for peace were not succeeding. World War II was tearing apart both Europe and America, and thousands were dying.

Though founded by Christian pacifists, FOR was not explicitly Christian. However, as the war continued, the small Kansas City branch felt the need for "a spiritual foundation to sustain their pacifism in the midst of wholesale carnage." They asked for help from the Wider Quaker Fellowship. The Quakers sent their chairwoman, Emma Cadbury, to Kansas City to organize a local Society of Friends, and the Penn Valley Friends was formed in 1942, a group that "would provide religious and ethical footings for several white civil rights activists."

> The small Kansas City branch felt the need for "a spiritual foundation to sustain their pacifism in the midst of wholesale carnage."

Once World War II was well underway in Europe, pacifists in FOR realized they couldn't stop the war. Instead of campaigning against war, they instead focused their efforts on local issues of peace, the most pressing of which was racial violence. They formed the Committee on the Practice of Democracy (COPOD), intentionally leaving words referring to race out of their title so as not to be inflammatory. The committee aimed to bring racial equality to Kansas City. At the first COPOD meeting, one of the few African Americans present was Girard T. Bryant, who originally came to Kansas City to teach at Western Baptist Bible College. Another Christian involved in COPOD and early desegregation was Ruth Gordon, a Quaker, who desegregated the University of Kansas Medical Center by hiring its first black staff member.

In the spring of 1944, COPOD held a Race Relations Institute, and the church was at the forefront. For the conference, "several hundred blacks and whites gathered at the Grand Avenue Temple in downtown Kansas City." The first day of the institute, a scientist taught about the lack of evidence that one race was inferior to another, and the next day a local clergyman spoke on "racism as a moral issue." Attendees also participated in service projects and lessons on nonviolent action. COPOD found these efforts successful, and afterwards they formed interracial teams who began visiting segregated establishments in Kansas City and talking to the owners about discrimination.

The next year, Baptist minister and COPOD member Rev. Lawrence Scott suggested they begin a Fellowship House, and in 1946 members of COPOD, FOR, and Penn Valley Meeting for the Religious Society of Friends purchased a large Victorian home that served as the Fellowship House, a place where they held "conferences on peace and international relations, a bureau of 'liberal' speakers, weekend camps for area students to study labor and race relations problems, and workshops on direct action projects in race relations." Having a house was vital, since public gathering places banned interracial socializing. The Fellowship House attracted people of African American, Hispanic, Asian, and white descent as they shared meals and discussed current events in a relaxed atmosphere free of the racial stiffness in the city. Although there were no instant, widespread results from COPOD's efforts, their small actions slowly reshaped public consciousness.

School Desegregation

On the Kansas side, change was underway as well. Esther Brown, a Jewish, Johnson County housewife from Merriam, Kansas, heard that the children of her African American maid went to a school where conditions were far worse than that of the local school for white students. Brown began a crusade for equal facilities, and when she met with an unresponsive school board, she took the issue to

Esther Brown (pictured with her husband Paul) crusaded for black students to have equal educational facilities in Johnson County, Kansas.

court. The Kansas Supreme Court ruled in her favor, paving the way for national school desegregation five years later in the 1954 US Supreme Court case, *Brown vs. Board of Education* (a different "Brown" than Esther Brown). In 1969 she received the Brotherhood Award from the Kansas City Chapter of the National Conference of Christians and Jews.

While Esther Brown was fighting segregation in Kansas, other people of faith on the Missouri side were living lives of influence too. Lucille Harris Bluford, a black writer from Kansas City who was active in her church, wanted to study journalism on the graduate level at the University of Missouri (MU) School of Journalism's graduate program. For her undergraduate degree, she had known she could not attend MU, since the state universities were highly segregated. Black students were expected to go to the historically black college, Lincoln University. However, Lincoln University did not offer journalism. Bluford went instead to the University of Kansas Lawrence and graduated in 1932 with high honors. She later worked for the *Kansas City Call*, an African American-owned newspaper, where she eventually advanced to editor and publisher.

Churchgoer Lucille Bluford challenged the University of Missouri's segregation policy when she was denied entrance to the journalism program because of her race.

In 1939, when she wanted to attend graduate school, she applied to the University of Missouri School of Journalism's graduate program. She was accepted, but when she arrived in Columbia to enroll, she was turned away because of her race. They had not known she was African American. She filed a lawsuit against the university, and her case advanced to the Supreme Court of Missouri, which ruled in 1941 that if the black college, Lincoln University, could not offer a similar course, MU must admit Bluford. After the ruling, MU shut down its graduate-level journalism program, claiming it could not adequately operate with so many of its

KANSAS CITY LEGACY

Harold Roe Bartle

"THE RIGHTEOUS WILL BE REMEMBERED FOREVER..." PSALM 112:6

Driving north on Interstate 35 into Kansas City, you can see the skyline marked by the four pillars of Bartle Hall with modern sculptures sitting atop each one. The Kansas City Convention Center was nicknamed "Bartle Hall" in honor of Harold Roe Bartle, who served Kansas City as mayor from 1956 to 1963. While Bartle became most famous for his role as mayor, his other occupations included lawyer, banker, cattleman, college president, and public speaker.

Bartle was an active member of his church, Central Presbyterian Church, although perhaps a better way to phrase it would be, he was active in many churches throughout the city. His fellow church members commented on his numerous absences, since other churches frequently called on Bartle to fill in on a Sunday morning when their own pastor was sick. His daughter later wrote in a biography, "If Bartle was called to substitute for a pastor who was ill, he needed only the time to dress and get to the church. He could work out the sermon on the way."

Beyond preaching, Bartle also served the Presbyterian church as president of the Missouri Valley College, a Presbyterian college in Marshall, Missouri.

Bartle left behind several namesakes. The Convention Center was dubbed Bartle Hall in his honor. Bartle's nickname was "The Chief," and in 1962 owner Lamar Hunt named Kansas City's football team "the Chiefs," in honor of the mayor.

In an interview for a Johnson County newspaper, *The Squire*, Bartle said, "I've done what I wanted to do and for those I wanted to do it for. Nobody can ask for more."

Bartle Hall was named after Kansas City's famous mayor, Harold Roe Bartle

Mayor Bartle, an active member of the Presbyterian church, frequently preached for churches throughout the city.

professors and students engaged in World War II. Bluford never attended MU but continued to write for *The Call* in Kansas City. Over forty years later, in 1989, MU gave her an honorary doctorate.

Blockbusting and the Flight to the Suburbs

In the 1950s and 1960s, as the city expanded into suburbs, churches followed suit. Dave Davies, a gift planning advisor with Wycliffe Bible Translators, remembers that during his childhood in the 1960s, paved roads in Kansas City only went as far south as Ninety-Fifth Street. There was no Interstate 435 looping around the city, connecting the suburbs to each other. But in the 1960s, growth took off. The city grew to the south and the suburban population skyrocketed.

Not only did suburbs grow because of natural expansion, but they also grew because of segregation. As the city laws started forcing integrated education and housing, those who resisted integration moved to the suburbs.

With integration and the Fair Housing Act, the "white flight" phenomenon occurred across America as white families fled integrated inner cities and moved to the suburbs. Kansas City families joined this nationwide trend. According to an article by Benson Law, "Between 1958 and 1973, sixty thousand whites moved out of Kansas City and were replaced by about fifty thousand blacks believing they were moving into integrated neighborhoods. The neighborhoods were soon all black, as were the schools that served them."

As neighborhoods started integrating, a trend called blockbusting emerged. According to anthropologist Nathaniel Bozarth, an illegitimate realtor would watch for a white family moving off a block. The realtor would buy the first home that went up for sale and find a black family to move into the house, telling the family they were moving into an integrated neighborhood. Since black families couldn't get traditional mortgages, they would purchase the houses directly from the realtor, who would inflate the price and charge high interest rates. Then the black families would often default on the unreasonably high loan, and the realtor would get to keep the house.

Moreover, as soon as the black family moved onto a block, the realtor would go door-to-door creating fear among the surrounding white home owners that their housing value would now plummet and that they needed to sell their house as soon as possible. The homeowners would all sell their houses at a discounted price to the realtor. The realtor would then sell the houses at inflated prices to black families and the cycle would continue.

When blockbusting occurred in Kansas City, two prominent church leaders spoke out against the practice: Father A. James Blumeyer, the dean of Rockhurst University; and Dr. Robert Meneilly, pastor of Village Presbyterian Church in Prairie Village.

Father Blumeyer saw blockbusting working its way farther and farther south through Kansas City. As blockbusting encroached on the neighborhood where Rockhurst University was located, he worked to stop this trend. The 49/63 Neighborhood Coalition formed to protect the neighborhood from Forty-Ninth Street south of the Plaza, down to Sixty-Third Street, with its barriers stretching from Oak Street on the west to the Paseo on the east. As part of the 49/63 Neighborhood Coalition, Blumeyer went door-to-door throughout the neighborhood petitioning residents not to move out when black residents moved onto their block. He encouraged them not to be afraid of black people.

The second church leader, Meneilly, preached a sermon that caused such a stir that it was reprinted in the local paper. Meneilly started as Village Presbyterian Church's founding pastor when the church opened in 1949. Most new church plants at the time started by meeting in schools or theaters and later moved into a building once they could afford the construction costs. However, the real estate agreements of Prairie Village, a planned community by J. C. Nichols, required that churches only hold services in designated church buildings. So the Presbyterian churches around the area donated $100,000 for the construction of Village Presbyterian Church. According to the church's website, "They also sent an emerging young minister, Robert H. Meneilly, to spread the good news about

Dr. Robert Meneilly (pictured with his wife Shirley and son Robert) urged his congregation to let go of prejudice and embrace equal housing.

this village church. When the last bricks were set in place, Bob and his wife, Shirley, had already built a congregation with their year-long house-to-house visitation." On the first Sunday the church's doors opened, 282 people attended.

Throughout his career as a minister, Meneilly spoke out against blockbusting and urged his congregation to love everyone. On February 14, 1965, he delivered the sermon "I Trouble—Segregating God." The local newspaper, *The Country Squire*, reprinted it "[b]ecause the sermon caused quite a bit of comment in the area . . ."

> "Prayer and prejudice can never dwell in the same heart."
>
> -Dr. Robert Meneilly

Meneilly's sermon claimed that congregants could not be Christian and ignore the issue of race, saying "Prayer and prejudice can never dwell in the same heart." Meneilly pressed his congregation to admit their prejudice and "let the Negro move into our beautiful community—after all, it is God's—not ours."

He asked them to stop depending on legislation to bring about civil rights and start taking personal responsibility to love all races. Regarding blockbusting, he encouraged his congregation not to give into "panic selling" when a black family moved in. He preached, "We must insure democracy of housing in this community whatever our inbred emotions may say about it. We must act on our Christian convictions—not our pagan prejudices."

In addition to creating enough of a stir to be printed in the local paper, the controversial sermon also sparked backlash for Meneilly in the form of threats directed toward both him and his children. However, he kept preaching love for everyone, and his congregation supported him during the opposition.

Despite the efforts of Blumeyer and Meneilly, blockbusting continued. Moreover, the racial shift was reflected among churches in the Kansas City metro area. As families who could afford the transition moved out to the suburbs, the city's churches relocated to the suburbs as well. According to Zach Daughtrey, historian for the Kansas City Diocese, the only churches who stayed in the city instead of moving to the suburbs were the Catholic churches and the black churches. The segregation continued into future decades and to this day shapes the landscape of churches in Kansas City.

Celebrating the Good

We record this section of history with a heavy heart. It should not have happened. Though some church members did speak out, the majority did not. This chapter feels like a gaping hole where there should have been a church movement but where there was none. We acknowledge the pain, the injustice, and the lack of attention given to what should have been a prominent issue.

Yet we celebrate the pockets of church members who worked to pave the way for the civil rights movement that followed decades down the road. Lucille Bluford refused to take no for an answer when she was turned away from the University of Missouri. Esther Brown insisted all children in her community should receive equal education. Nelson Crews spoke up about the inconsistency of those who claimed to be Christian yet refused to allow an African American Bible college to enter their neighborhood. Father Blumeyer and Dr. Meneilly used their pulpits to encourage the city to stay put instead of running away from what they feared. Church leaders from both races came together in the Citizen's League, and this group may have prevented race riots from breaking out in Kansas City like they did in nearby cities the summer of 1919. And finally, the Fellowship of Reconciliation recognized that true racial healing begins at the dinner table, and they brought races together in their homes.

These heroes came before the civil rights movement began. Their faithful service preserved Kansas City from becoming worse than it could have been. They faced death threats, bombings, and criticism from the public. Yet they persevered. The initiative of the few often paves the way for the majority to follow. God used Kansas City as an instigator for social change. The city became a place for new ideas to grow and a venue for reform.

While the parents were busy moving to the suburbs, the youth were ripe for a revolution of their own, one that spanned racial barriers and brought new life to the city.

Chapter 8
Taking Back the Youth
(1940 - 1980)

Along with the civil rights movement, the Jesus movement swept through the nation during the 1960s and 1970s. It began on the West Coast and made its way across America, even spanning the Atlantic Ocean to impact the United Kingdom. During the Jesus movement, young people, many of them former hippies, turned to Jesus by the thousands. However, just as the civil rights movement only came after decades of groundwork to prepare public consciousness for the revolution, the same was true of the Jesus movement. In Kansas City, the movement's roots could be traced back to the 1940s, an era when there were no youth groups, an era that found Kansas City in the thick of war.

With the Pendergast machine finally ousted, Kansas City opened the 1940s in recovery mode, maintaining their Clean Sweep Crusade to rid government of corrupt politicians and rebuilding their economy from the Great Depression. When the bombs hit Pearl Harbor, the United States jumped into World War II, and Kansas City dove into the war effort full force. Factories sprang up manufacturing everything from camouflage paint to aircraft engines. "By many accounts this was the most active civil defense response of any inland US city," according to *Kansas City: An American Story*.

Youthfront Begins

As fathers went off to war and mothers joined the workforce, the war began to take a toll on the nation's families. A 1942 issue of *Elementary School Journal* coined the term "latchkey children" to describe youth whose parents were absent. With fathers at war and mothers at work, crime among youth increased in Kansas City, and "burglaries, car thefts and truancy zoomed in Kansas City," according to *Kansas City: An American Story*. "A gang called the Clan broke windows in the Country Club district" and young women's "delinquency rate" climbed 300 percent higher than before the war, their main offense being "short-lived romances with soldiers passing through town." Dads and older brothers were off fighting the war, and the youth lacked the supervision and role models former generations had benefited from. Kansas City, along with the rest of the nation, worried about its young people. In the 1940s, few churches had full-time youth ministers serving the metro area. To fill this need, many youth ministries began across the nation, including Young Life, Fellowship of Christian Athletes, and Youth for Christ.

Hundreds of youth attend Al and Vidy Metsker's second youth rally, "Singspiration," which later became Kansas City Youth for Christ.

Against this backdrop, Al Metsker and his wife, Vidy, held the first Kansas City Youth for Christ rally in 1943. Al and Vidy shared a passion for youth ministry, having come to Christ through a youth program years earlier. During his own teenage years, Al Metsker came to Kansas City to work in the factories for the war. He had a deferment, so he couldn't go to war. He started attending Central Bible Church and became a Christian under its pastor, Dr. Walter Wilson, who founded Kansas City Bible College (now Calvary University). The church had a vivacious youth program, a feature almost unheard of at the time. Al met Vidy at the church, and they got married. Since both Al and Vidy had heard the gospel for the first time as teenagers, after they got married, they each had a burden to reach teenagers. So the Metskers invited young people from area churches to a youth rally. For their first rally on June 19, 1943, one hundred fifty youth came. They called it "Singspiration," singing not just hymns but also Christian choruses (an edgy and progressive move at the time). The youth loved the rally and asked the Metskers to hold another one the next month. The rallies continued, and at the third meeting, one thousand students attended.

"It was obvious that God was doing a work," Vidy said later in an interview. "Our whole goal was trying to reach students with the gospel, and we just followed God when He told us something to do."

The meetings drew youth from many church congregations, and the meetings helped get rid of sectarianism, since the youth rallies spanned denominations. Across the nation, similar youth ministries started. In 1947, they formed an official board and united as one organization, Youth for Christ International. Their first staff member, Billy Graham, frequently visited Kansas City to speak at youth rallies. By the 1950s, Kansas City Youth for Christ was holding weekly Saturday night rallies. They added Bible studies and counseling ministries. In the 1960s they added a sixteen hundred-person auditorium to their building and a TV studio in 1978.

> "It was obvious that God was doing a work. . . . [W]e just followed God when He told us something to do."
>
> -Vidy Metsker

An enthusiastic Cliff Barrows leads the singing for a Youth for Christ banquet at Linwood Presbyterian Church. Billy Graham and Al Metsker are seated on the front row.

COURTESY OF YOUTHFRONT AND VIDY METSKER

The first board for Youth for Christ International included Al Metsker (front row, far right) and Billy Graham (to his right).

Then and Now

Kansas City Youth for Christ changed its name to Youthfront, and today—over seventy-five years later—the ministry continues to reach thousands of youth in the Kansas City metro area through camps, mission trips, and local ministry. Current Youthfront director Mike King says that since the time of its founding, at least three hundred thousand students have gone through its programs. From Youthfront's programs have come other well-known ministries in Kansas City such as The Sending Project started by Eric Rochester and PastorServe led by Jimmy Dodd.

The Jesus Movement in Kansas City

The second root of Kansas City's Jesus movement also began in the 1940s. But this root could be traced back to sunny Los Angeles. At the far western edge of the country, Dr. Henrietta Mears was teaching a Sunday school class for Hollywood Presbyterian Church. That class would spark Kansas City's chapter of the Jesus movement, as well as the birth of many organizations in Kansas City, including the International House of Prayer, Ichthus campus ministry, Shelterwood, and others.

Mears had a passion for discipling her students, and one of her Sunday school pupils at Hollywood Presbyterian was Bill Bright. As a seminary student at Princeton and Fuller Theological Seminaries, Bright felt called to begin campus outreach at the University of

California at Los Angeles (UCLA). The first college student Bright discipled was Ted Nissen, who later moved to Kansas City to become the head pastor of Colonial Presbyterian Church. Bright met Nissen in the late 1940s, and together they started a campus ministry at UCLA. In 1951, the ministry became "Campus Crusade for Christ." This ministry continues today as "Cru" and reaches millions of people worldwide.

Meanwhile in Kansas City in 1964, Colonial Presbyterian Church was looking for a new lead pastor. By this time, Nissen was an assistant pastor at Bellaire Presbyterian Church in California. From Mears's Sunday school class, a web of relationships connected Nissen to a member of Colonial in Kansas City. Nissen was friends with Jim Rayburn, who started Young Life ministries. Rayburn lived in LA, but his brother lived in Kansas City and attended Colonial. So the brother called Rayburn, Rayburn called Nissen, and Nissen agreed to come and pastor Colonial.

Ted Nissen pastored at Colonial Presbyterian Church for thirty-seven years.

COURTESY OF BOB LEHEITNER

Soon after Nissen arrived at Colonial, he recognized that they needed a youth pastor, so he hired Richard Beach, a Campus Crusade for Christ staff missionary who shared the same philosophies for ministry. They had a vision for discipleship groups and sharing the gospel. As Beach began the youth group, hundreds of students from around Kansas City flocked to Colonial each night of the week.

Dave Davies, a gift planning advisor with Wycliffe Bible

COURTESY OF BOB LEHEITNER

Richard Beach (pictured on left with Bob Lehleitner) attracted hundreds of students to Colonial's youth group.

DISCOVERING THE PAST TO SHAPE OUR FUTURE

Audiences flowed onto the field of Municipal Stadium during Billy Graham's 1967 revivals in Kansas City.

Billy Graham Crusades

When Kansas City built the Convention Hall back in 1899, the hall was opened in February, but it was not filled to capacity until D. L. Moody's revivals. A similar thing happened when the Chiefs came to Kansas City in 1963. Their opening game of the 1966 football season brought in over forty-three thousand people to Municipal Stadium, which served for both Kansas City's baseball and football games. The stadium was not filled to capacity until the following year in September 1967 for Billy Graham's ten-day evangelistic crusade.

The first evening opened with over thirty-two thousand people, and the crowds kept growing. The next day brought in forty-two thousand, and the *Kansas City Star* reported, "Yesterday's crowd was the largest using the stadium since the Chiefs' opening game October 2, 1966, when 43,885 persons attended. As the stands filled to capacity, ushers directed the crowd to places outside the baselines and in the outfield. In the bleachers, parents held their youngsters to make room for other adults."

Crowds continued to grow over the ten-day period of revival sermons, until Graham brought in "53,000 in one record-setting night" according to the *Star*. Overall, the campaign reached 364,000 people.

CHAPTER 8

Like Moody, Graham preached a simple message of salvation through belief in Jesus. Also similar to Moody, Graham provided an opportunity for audience members to commit their lives to Jesus.

"At the close of every day of the crusade," the Star wrote, "Graham invited people down to his podium at second base to publicly welcome Christ into their hearts. Thousands responded."

He also encouraged the people of Kansas City that they were a unique city unparalleled in religious background. "There are no people in America better equipped to help lead the nation back to God than the people of Kansas and Missouri," Graham said.

> *"There are no people in America better equipped to help lead the nation back to God than the people of Kansas and Missouri."*
>
> -Billy Graham

COURTESY OF YOUTHFRONT AND VIDY METSKER

The revival's steering committee gathered on the field of Municipal Stadium.

Translators who grew up in Kansas City, recalls a Thursday night during the summer in 1974. He was in high school, had just come to Christ through a Fellowship of Christian Athletes (FCA) camp in Colorado, and was eagerly sharing the gospel with anyone who would listen. While working a lifeguarding job, he was talking to a fellow lifeguard, who also happened to be a believer.

"You need to come to Colonial," she said.

He did and was shocked at what he saw. He arrived at ten thirty on a Thursday night mid-summer. There were no programs, nothing officially going on at the church, yet hundreds of students filled the sprawling parking lot and spilled over onto the property next door. There were conversations going on about the Bible, and students huddled together praying. The Jesus movement was in full swing at Colonial.

Colonial's group was just one example of a citywide phenomenon. Across the metro area, as the youth came to Christ, they took the radical, free-spirited hippie culture and channeled it toward Him.

The Charismatic Movement

The charismatic movement was a churchwide phenomenon that exploded during the 1960s and 1970s, and Kansas City was touched by it as well. Down the road from Colonial Presbyterian Church stood another church, Second Presbyterian Church at Fifty-fifth Street and Oak in Kansas City. Second Presbyterian Church housed the Agape ministries, an outreach program started by David Rose, a former drug addict. The beginnings of this ministry also can be traced to California.

Rose, a Kansas City native from Independence, Missouri, moved to southern California at age sixteen, completely entrenched in hippie culture and the lifestyle of drug addiction. Through a long series of events that included his arrest for distributing LSD, he received a Bible in jail and started praying for God to help him. He was released from prison and returned to the drug lifestyle. But while in California, he received a gospel tract, read the tract, and gave his life to the Lord. After moving to Berkeley, California, and working with the Christian World Liberation Front, Rose came back to Kansas City and in 1969 started a ministry called Agape that quickly grew to several thousand people.

Second Presbyterian lent its basement to the Agape meetings. Agape was a flood of former hippies who had turned to Christ.

Around seven hundred people crowded the basement of Second Presbyterian Church each week for the Agape meetings. They spoke in tongues, worshiped, and prophesied.

An article from *The Pitch* shares a memory Reverend David Altschul recalls from going to a meeting when he was a teenager. A man had been injured from a motorcycle accident, and another man extended his hand to the injured man and said, "In the name of Jesus Christ of Nazareth, rise up and walk." According to Altschul, the man did.

> *"In the name of Jesus Christ of Nazareth, rise up and walk."*

Then and Now

Altschul went on to study at Full Faith Bible College in 1973, became an ordained minister, and years later started Reconciliation Ministries on Troost Avenue, which continues today as the nonprofit Reconciliation Services.

Frank Brown, who later helped found Servant Foundation, the charitable foundation in Kansas City now known as The Signatry, recalls those early days. Coming from earlier attending an Episcopalian Church, he was not ready for speaking in tongues or any of the more "spirit-filled" gifts, as the movement referred to them. But his daughter started going to some strange Jesus-hippy group in a church basement, so he went to see what the hubbub was. He got "hooked on Jesus," as he would later refer to it. During the peak of Agape ministries, there were several thousand people involved.

Ichthus Ministries

Back at Colonial Presbyterian Church, by 1971 Richard Beach had brought the youth group to an attendance of fifteen hunddred students. People involved in the youth group would later start movements across Kansas City, such as Mike Bickle who started the International House of Prayer in Grandview, Missouri. Bickle had a similar story to Dave Davies of coming to Christ in high school during the Jesus movement. Bickle grew up at Eighty-fifth and Paseo in what he describes as a "crime-infested, low-income

International Charismatic Conference

In July 1977, fifty thousand Christians filled Arrowhead Stadium for the International Charismatic Conference, a major step forward on the road to Christian unity. According to Rev. Dr. Vinson Synan, a Pentecostal leader and planning committee member, "The [Charismatic] movement reached a climax in America around 1977 during the Kansas City Conference, because all the different streams came together." Baptists, Catholics, Episcopalians, Lutherans, and many other denominations gathered together to worship and listen to speakers from the different denominations.

The main theme of the conference was "Jesus is Lord," and speakers emphasized that no matter the denomination, they were all "one in the Spirit." Featured speakers included Maria Von Trapp (whose life inspired the musical, *The Sound of Music*) and President Jimmy Carter's sister, Ruth Carter Stapleton.

Larry Christenson, a Lutheran Charismatic revival leader, preached that revival was not a means to "bolster denominational programs." He said, "The Lord has not brought this renewal to prop up and bless the status quo. He has brought it to advance his program, which is to make us one as He and the Father are one."

OCTOBER 1977
THE INTERNATIONAL MAGAZINE
DEDICATED TO CHRISTIAN GROWTH

new wine

CHARLES SIMPSON MINISTRIES

Jesus Exalted

The Government of God • Baxter • 4
What God Wants Now • Basham • 14
The Beauty of Holiness • Mumford • 25
What God Wants Next • Prince • 34
God Can Use Anybody • Simpson • 40

The October 1977 cover of New Wine magazine featured Kansas City's International Charismatic Conference, a gathering that attracted fifty thousand Christians from across the world to Arrowhead Stadium.

neighborhood." His father was an international champion boxer who claimed no religion, and Bickle grew up going to the bars with his dad. As a sophomore in high school, Bickle recalls his varsity football coach, a leader in FCA, inviting Bickle to his house for a Bible study. Bickle had no greater hero than his football coach, so he went. Through the study, Bickle gave his life to Christ. His coach was an elder at Colonial Presbyterian, so Bickle started attending the burgeoning youth group.

A couple years later, Bickle and his friend Steve Smalley attended Colonial's Ichthus summer program. As two soon-to-be seniors, they wanted to spend their last summer in high school for the Lord. They lived in a discipleship house with Bob Lehleitner. Bob was at the time in college himself and later became a pastor at Colonial. Lehleitner took the two students under his wing. He discipled them, studied the Bible with them, and taught them to share the gospel with others.

Bob Lehleitner (center) discipled Dr. Steve Smalley (left) and Mike Bickle (right) during Colonial's summer program, Ichthus.

The summer was powerful, and Bickle and his friend returned to their high school football team ready to make a difference. After playing each game, they would rush the stands, sign autographs for junior high students, and invite them to the Ichthus ministry house to hang out after the game. By the end of the school year, they had a hundred students coming each Friday night. Bickle told his co-leaders, "The last Friday of the school year, I'm going to present the gospel to them." Bickle did just that, and all one hundred students stood to receive Christ.

Students gather in the Ichthus House for Colonial's student ministry.

It seemed that wherever Bickle went, he brought revival with him. He went to Washington University in St. Louis to play football and started three Bible studies during his first three weeks there. After a year there, he returned to Kansas City to help his brother who had broken his neck. Once his brother had stabilized the next year, Bickle started college again. This time he went to the University of Missouri, Columbia, and played on the football team. "I'm going to unite all the Christians at Mizzou," Lehleitner recalled Bickle saying. Lehleitner shared in an interview that at the time, he was skeptical, but sure enough, Bickle went to MU and within a couple months had forty students meeting at his dorm each week. At MU, Bickle decided to witness to every person he saw. He regularly skipped class to share the gospel with students, and he only came to class for the tests, yet he still earned A's in his classes.

This student group soon turned into five hundred people and became Ichthus Campus Ministries. In its peak, Ichthus had nineteen groups on campuses throughout the Midwest, facilitated by Kansas City's Mike Bickle, Bob Lehleitner, and others who were involved in Young Life and then the subsequent Ichthus groups.

By 1980, Richard Beach had begun a ministry at Colonial Presbyterian called Doulos, and out of this ministry came Shelterwood, a residential treatment agency for teens in Independence, Missouri. Through Doulos, Beach mentored college students "in life, leadership, and the teachings of Jesus." A board member of the ministry had a teenage daughter who was struggling, and the board member asked if she could stay with the college students in the Doulos program. Beach agreed, and the daughter's life was transformed through their mentorship combined with professional therapy. Impressed by his daughter's transformation, the father encouraged Beach to open the program to other teens. The ministry eventually turned into Shelterwood, a residential treatment agency for troubled teens.

Then and Now

Nearly forty years later, Shelterwood has helped thousands of families throughout the Kansas City area. Colonial's summer internship program also continues today, and approximately one thousand students have served as interns. Of those thousand students, four hundred have continued into full-time ministry.

Lessons from a Movement

The Jesus movement wasn't the first time a spiritual awakening swept across America, and it won't be the last. Spiritual revivals have regularly occurred in America over the past few centuries. We can learn valuable lessons from the last movement in order to bring about another movement just like it.

First, we can be faithful in the small acts of service. Kansas City's youth revival had humble beginnings—a youth pastor led a couple students to Christ. Those students later held a youth rally, with no idea it would take off and become Youth for Christ and later Youthfront. Separately, another Sunday school teacher out in California, Henrietta Mears, faithfully discipled her students. She taught them to follow Jesus, not knowing the impact she would have. One of her students, Bill Bright, discipled Ted Nissen; Nissen discipled Richard Beach, and Kansas City is still feeling the payoff from those investments. Little efforts go a long way. The small beginnings start major movements.

Second, don't shy away from the difficult. We can easily romanticize the Jesus movement days, when thousands of students came to Christ. But in actuality, it was messy. Pastor Bob Lehleitner tells stories of breaking up fights and picking up old cigarettes from the parking lot the morning after an outreach. Second Presbyterian Church allowed their basement to be filled week after week with hippies and drug addicts seeking Jesus. Churches during the Jesus movement offered the gospel to all kinds of people, and all kinds of people responded. Looking back, we can see the fruit and package it up in a tidy basket labeled "the Jesus movement." But in the moment, there was chaos, late nights, and the uncertainty of inviting friends to Bible studies and sharing the gospel, not knowing how they would respond.

Third, churches were receptive to the big initiatives. They hosted over fifty-three thousand people in one night at the Billy Graham Crusade. They allowed hundreds of students to hang out in their church parking lots or basements on any night of the week, and happily put in the work to maintain housing and facilities. They were faithful in the small things and prepared for the large movements. Out of the radical dedication of the Jesus movement came many organizations that are well-known in Kansas City today: Cru, International House of Prayer of Kansas City (IHOPKC), FCA, Ichthus college ministry, and hundreds of others. Forty years later, their ministries still stand. Thousands have come to Christ, and the

Christian landscape of Kansas City has been permanently changed. Let's learn from them to be faithful at whatever act of service God puts before us, embrace the chaos of growth, and be ready for God to do big things.

Just as the Civil War followed the Second Great Awakening, so the civil rights movement came alongside the Jesus movement. Social reform often follows on the heels of spiritual awakening. Change brings about more change. Such was the case for Kansas City the spring of 1968.

Chapter 9
Freedom Marches and Riots

(1968)

One chilly April evening in Memphis, Dr. Martin Luther King Jr., stepped out onto his hotel room balcony. The day before, he had delivered his famous "Mountaintop Speech" at Mason Temple, and this evening, he and his friends were leaving to dine with a local minister. When King stepped outside, his friend called from below reminding him to bring a coat. Before King had time to turn around, a gunshot sounded. The echoes of that gunshot would reverberate across the nation.

The days following King's assassination pulled Kansas City's churches into the civil rights movement in a way they never dreamed. As violence erupted across Kansas City, church leaders from all races and denominations worked together with city officials to restore order.

Riots Begin

King was assassinated on April 4, 1968, the Thursday before Palm Sunday. The school district of Kansas City, Kansas, dealt differently with the turmoil than its counterpart school district in Missouri. Reverend David K. Fly, a white priest who had recently been ordained as clergy at Grace and Holy Trinity Episcopal Cathedral in Kansas City, Missouri, recounts his memories of that week. On Friday, the day after the assassination, students from Kansas's high schools wanted to march downtown. The superintendent came to the school and marched with the students. He also called the chief of police from Kansas City, Kansas, and asked for their senior black officer to join the march. They all marched downtown, there were a few speeches, and then they returned to the school for a school-sponsored memorial service. Missouri schools, however, continued as usual.

After the assassination, city and church officials set aside Palm Sunday for a march commemorating King. That Sunday, fifteen thousand people from both the Kansas and Missouri sides peacefully marched in his memory. They grieved the death of King and prayed for reconciliation.

King's funeral took place the following Tuesday. Again, schools on the Kansas side closed that Tuesday so that students could stay home and watch the funeral. Schools on the Missouri side stayed open. The superintendent had announced that weekend that under no circumstances would schools close the next week; then he left town on a business trip. Students were irate. Fly recalls,

The students' anger and frustration built; some ran through the hallways in the schools kicking over trash cans. The school authorities in some cases called the police, and they responded. And, in a couple of situations sprayed Mace on the students. The news that classes weren't going to be cancelled spread like wildfire as more and more kids left school and ran through the hallways of other schools encouraging students to join them. The kids poured out of the schools and into the streets.

Meanwhile, the city's clergy were gathering that morning for a peaceful memorial service. Fly, the Dean of Grace and Holy Trinity Cathedral, joined with the leadership of the Metropolitan Inter-Church Agency (MICA) to organize a memorial service for the day of King's funeral. MICA was a large group of Protestant and Catholic ministers in Kansas City who worked closely together to serve the city. All denominations joined together for the service. However, the service was soon interrupted by an emergency call from the National Association for the Advancement of Colored People (NAACP).

"At one point I looked up to see a member of the altar guild frantically waving their hands at me and mouthing the words, 'Emergency, emergency,'" Fly said. "When I entered the sacristy I was given a message for our Assistant Bishop Robert Spears . . . who got on the phone and was told that unruly crowds of kids were leaving school and beginning to march towards downtown. The NAACP representative asked that the clergy gathered for the service go immediately to the scene to try to organize the march and to attempt to keep things cool."

The students had left schools by the hundreds and were gathering for a protest march. The NAACP representative called asking clergy to stop the service, go to the march, and try to keep it from becoming violent. Clergy immediately ended the service and strategized what to do. Some went to City Hall, the destination of the march, while others went to the marchers' current location.

At the scene of the chaos, the clergy found themselves on the front lines, literally, as they linked arms and led the march. The students marched downtown, but they were blocked by a police barricade at Paseo and Interstate 70. The marchers insisted on going downtown, but the police had received strict instructions from the chief of police not to allow the students to go any further.

While the students were arguing to be allowed through the barricade, Mayor Ilus W. Davis arrived. Mayor Davis, a member of Country Club Christian Church, had worked to pass a fair housing ordinance for Kansas City. City officials resisted the ordinance, but it ended up being superseded by the US Government's Fair Housing Act in 1968. Mayor Davis attempted to join in the march and lead the students up Paseo. However, two policemen grabbed his arms and led him back into the police car. Seeing how the police treated the mayor further upset the student marchers, and they bolted through the police barricades and ran down I-70 toward downtown.

Frantically trying to keep the peace, the city leaders hastily organized a demonstration on the steps of City Hall. Once the march reached City Hall, they held speeches. In order to occupy the students, the church leaders planned a dance to take place at Holy Name Catholic Church, at Twenty-third and Benton. They coordinated buses to transport the students to the church.

However, while they were still downtown after the speeches, a bottle was thrown from someone in the crowd, hitting an officer. The police began throwing canisters of tear gas into the crowd. The crowds ran. Fly was with Father Ed Warner, a black priest who was the rector of St. Augustine's Episcopal Church in Kansas City, when the riot erupted. The police stopped Warner to search him. Fly recalls the events:

Father Warner (clergy on left) and Reverend Fly (clergy on right) converse after the civil rights march to City Hall. Clergy were at the forefront of the march.

Father Warner falls to the pavement in front of police, and Reverend Fly runs to his aid.

I heard Father Warner say, "Wait a minute, I'm a Priest of the Church. I'm on your side." I ran over to Ed, as he tried to talk to the officer, but the police knocked him to the pavement with a club. Tear gas was beginning to billow around us. Two other officers grabbed me, and I was struck twice in the chest with a club. I went down like a rock. I tried to crawl away, but was overcome by the tear gas. . . . The next thing I heard was the voice of a young black man who screamed, "Hey, a brother is down!" The nicest words I had ever heard in my life.

> "Hey, a brother is down!"

Five young black men carried Fly to a car belonging to a reporter from a local news station. As the reporter drove to the hospital, he asked Fly if they could stop by Holy Name Church.

Back at the church, as the dance was underway, Fly recalls the horrific scene that unfolded. He watched as police surrounded the church, blocked the doorways, and then threw cans of tear gas into the basement.

"I can still hear the screams of the kids as they were trapped inside the church," Fly said. "It was a horrible scene."

Churches Work for Peace

Throughout the city, violence escalated as students returned home to their neighborhoods and told others what had happened. Amid the violence, Kansas City churches stayed active trying to maintain peace.

That same Tuesday evening, the city enacted a 7 p.m. curfew, and so many black citizens were arrested for being out past curfew that the jails filled to overflowing. MICA arranged for churches to hold the overflow. The police would drop the young people who had been arrested off at the churches and cathedrals. Fly recalls telling youth who had been arrested and dropped off at Grace and Holy Trinity, "Look, we're not a jail. You can leave if you want. If you leave, you'll probably get arrested, so you can sleep the night here. We have cots. We have bologna sandwiches from the Salvation Army. So take a rest and have a sandwich." People from local seminaries came to help deal with the students who had been arrested. Staff and volunteers from MICA took statements from the youth on how the police had treated them, and MICA also provided volunteer clergy to go to police precincts as watchers, both to protect those who had been arrested and to ensure the police were not falsely accused of abuse.

In the days following the riot, churches worked with the radio and television stations, city officials, and the school district to restore order. Many pastors took an active role in this process, including Pastor Charles Briscoe of the Paseo Baptist Church and Pastor Wallace S. Hartfield Sr. of the Metropolitan Missionary Baptist Church.

Lehleitner, then a college student at UMKC and member of Colonial Presbyterian Church, recalls seeing the riots firsthand. He and his friends drove to see the riots. They saw fires, people breaking windows to rob stores—Lehleitner and his friends turned around right away!

Nissen, the head pastor of Colonial Presbyterian Church, was good friends with Briscoe of Paseo Baptist Church. Colonial was predominantly white, and Paseo Baptist, predominantly black. The two pastors brought their congregations together and prayed. They were scared, according to Lehleitner. The congregations decided to go together and march in the inner city, hand in hand, alternating as white, black, white, black, marching down the road. Lehleitner shares that after that march, the city's riots calmed down.

> The congregations decided to go together and march in the inner city, hand in hand . . .

A couple months after the riot, churches formed the Kansas City Crisis Program, a group organized to create dialogue between black and white people and "to seek peaceful solutions to racial tensions." They met in churches and homes of church people. A young black social worker, Bob Jones, worked with Fly to coordinate the program. Jones did not attend church anywhere, and Fly recalls a conversation they had:

> I remember saying to him one time, "Bob, you're not a church member," I said. "Why are you putting all this energy into this program?" And, what he said to me was, "David, I believe a time is coming in our country when people will no longer have a forum in which they can speak civilly to one another." The church may be the only place where that dialogue takes place.

Looking back on the effect of the riots, Fly said, "It was an incredibly unified experience for all of us." Churches within the Kansas City area took an active role in stopping the marches and restoring order to the city.

Throughout the civil rights period, Kansas City area churches and their pastors were actively involved in other aspects of the desegregation movement. These included nonviolent peace marches, securing equal jobs and equal pay for workers and church members, school desegregation for students from area churches, and voter registration for church members and others.

The Value of Connection

Although heartbreaking for Kansas City, the riots offered churches a chance to shine as they pulled together and helped the city through a moment of crisis. The churches succeeded in supporting the city because long before the crisis hit, they had built connections with each other, with outside organizations, and with city officials.

KANSAS CITY LEGACY
• • •
Emanuel Cleaver II
"THE RIGHTEOUS WILL BE REMEMBERED FOREVER..." PSALM 112:6

In September of 1977, a major flood of Brush Creek led to severe damage in Kansas City, especially the Country Club Plaza. KMBC News counted twenty-five deaths and estimated damages up to $100 million. Amid the havoc, once again the church rose to the challenge. Zion Grove Baptist Church stepped up to help flood victims, and the first federally coordinated effort to aid the flood victims met in their church. In a news report the week following the flood, KMBC News said of the church, "It is the Zion Grove Baptist Church that has become the main headquarters for Kansas City's efforts to pull itself out of this week's disaster."

Emanuel Cleaver, then pastor of St. James United Methodist Church, "testified to Congress about Kansas Citians jumping through hoops to get federal disaster aid." When he later became Kansas City's first African American mayor in 1991, he headed up a flood control project and earned a street named after him, Emanuel Cleaver II Boulevard, that runs along Brush Creek's north bank. Cleaver later went on to serve as congressman in the US House of Representatives.

Although the flood destroyed the area, it prompted a great renovation that helped the Plaza thrive. As usual, people from the church were closely tied to helping the city.

Named after Emanuel Cleaver II, the boulevard runs north of Brush Creek as part of a flood control project begun by Cleaver.

Congressman Cleaver pastored St. James United Methodist Church in Kansas City before beginning his political career.

Reading between the lines from Fly's account, we can discover much about the healthy relationships the churches maintained with the city. Churches worked with the city to plan a peaceful march on Palm Sunday in memory of Dr. Martin Luther King Jr. The following Tuesday, when the students began their impromptu march downtown, church leaders were in touch with the city's school bus system to arrange last-minute transportation for all those students from City Hall to Holy Name Catholic Church. And when the jails overflowed that night because of the city curfew, MICA coordinated with the city to allow churches to hold the overflow and to help record witnesses' stories. For all of these connections to take place, we can assume a healthy relationship of trust already existed between the city and the churches. In the city's time of crisis, it leaned on the church because the church had already earned its trust.

And not only city officials but outside organizations also trusted the church. The NAACP knew Kansas City's church leaders were peaceful and nonbiased. When the students left school to march downtown, the NAACP knew what number to call. They called the church.

Beyond good relations with the city and organizations, churches maintained close relationships with each other. Black and white, Protestant and Catholic—throughout the city, church leaders had already overcome barriers of race and denomination long before the riot broke out. They had already organized MICA as a way to work together and serve the city. And they had broken through racial barriers that the city was still trying to reconcile. Though different races, Reverend Fly and Father Warner were friends. When Warner was accosted by the police, Fly came to his aid. Similarly, pastors Charles Briscoe and Ted Nissen were close enough friends that when the riots hit the city, Briscoe and Nissen could quickly pull their diverse congregations together for prayer and a peaceful march.

The riots of 1968 illustrate how the church can support the city in a time of crisis. In order to be a support, churches must first build relational networks ahead of time—with each other, with city officials, and with outside organizations. The true value of these well-built networks is shown times of crisis, but the connections are built during times of peace.

Chapter 10

A New Millennium of Growth

(1984 - 2019)

The 1980s and 1990s brought exponential growth to Kansas City's suburbs. The population of Lee's Summit, Missouri, nearly tripled from 1980 to 2000, as forty-two thousand new residents moved to that suburb alone. On the Kansas side, the entire Johnson County population almost doubled, adding over one hundred eighty-four thousand residents to the county. As thousands of people moved to the suburbs, so did the churches. Zach Daughtrey, historian for the Kansas City Diocese, shared that Catholic churches and African American churches stayed in the urban core, but many other church denominations left and relocated in the suburbs. However, the next few decades would bring about new unity and collaboration among churches in Kansas City.

There was a swell of nondenominational churches starting up, and with them, house Bible studies. The charismatic movement and the Jesus movement left an impact on church culture across the United States. In Kansas City, a prayer movement started, sparking the growth of many new ministries across the metro area.

Preparing the City Through Prayer

In 1984, Marilyn Griffin started Ministries of New Life as a cross-denominational prayer and teaching ministry to churches in Kansas City.

"It's really a work that [the Lord] did," Griffin says about those early years of the ministry. She recalls times of night and day prayer, people getting up at five o'clock in the morning every day to pray, mixed with periods of fasting. "It was very unusual praying," Griffin says. "It really takes the Spirit to maintain that."

After a three-year season of intermittent prayer and fasting, Griffin felt God calling her to work to bring together Kansas City's pastors. She approached the pastors about holding a National Day of Prayer gathering for the city. They agreed, and after that first meeting, Griffin asked if the pastors would like to

Christians gather downtown in Bartle Hall on May 4, 1989, for the third annual National Day of Prayer meeting.

MINISTRIES OF NEW LIFE

DISCOVERING THE PAST TO SHAPE OUR FUTURE

start meeting monthly for prayer, if she provided the venue. Again, they said yes, and those monthly meetings became the Citywide Prayer Movement.

> *"As they heard each other pray, the walls between them began to break down."*
>
> – Marilyn Griffin

"We first had to take [the pastors] to a hotel because they wouldn't go in each other's churches," Griffin recalls. "Then as they heard each other pray, the walls between them began to break down. It was a beautiful thing to see how the Spirit then began to knit their hearts together."

The monthly meetings continued under Griffin's leadership for eight years, until she felt God asking her to transfer leadership to the pastors. The leadership mantle eventually fell on the shoulders of Gary Schmitz, who today leads the Citywide Prayer Movement. Ministries of New Life continues leading the city in prayer gatherings of repentance according to the Jewish calendar.

Griffin sees their ministry as a walk of obedience: "When He called me, I never even knew what all it would entail, but as you just walk out your life, He unfolds your assignment for you."

At a Citywide Prayer Movement breakfast, a speaker encourages mayors and pastors to invite Christ to Kansas City. Right: Attendees listen to his challenge.

THE SPIRITUAL ROOTS OF KANSAS CITY

A New Millennium, a New Era for Kansas City

As the Citywide Prayer Movement took flight, the turn of the millennium ushered in new growth and the birth of many organizations around the city. The birth and growth of these ministries matched a nationwide trend of new non-profit ministries being formed.

Within a span of two years, from 1999 to 2001, several local ministries emerged, including the International House of Prayer of Kansas City (IHOPKC), PastorServe, Character That Counts, The Signatry, and Unconventional Business Network, among others.

In 1999, after pastoring for twenty-three years, Mike Bickle founded IHOPKC in Grandview, Missouri, as a twenty-four-seven prayer room and a worldwide mission base. The ministry continues today, impacting people worldwide. IHOPKC is known around the world yet remains somewhat of a secret in Kansas City. Also in 1999, Jimmy and Sally Dodd started PastorServe, a ministry to strengthen pastors by offering them care through coaching, crisis support, and counseling. Dodd had served as a pastor himself for twenty years before starting this new ministry. As PastorServe and IHOPKC came to fruition at the turn of the millennium, several other ministries were born as well.

Character That Counts began in July 2000, founded by Rod Handley in Lee's Summit. At the time, Handley had been working for Fellowship of Christian Athletes (FCA) at their headquarters in Kansas City. He had worked for them for fifteen years and was senior vice president then. However, five years prior, in 1995 he wrote the book *Character Counts: Who's Counting Yours?* to encourage Christian growth through accountability. His speaking platform exploded, and he was soon filling his weekends with speaking engagements, conferences, and workshops. By 2000, it became apparent that he could no longer do both—fill the speaking engagements and work full-time, so he took a leap of faith, resigned from his job at FCA and launched the ministry Character That Counts. Since 2000, Handley has written over 25 books and has had at least 250 speaking engagements per year. Character That Counts started a community Bible study, Teaching Guys Infinite Wisdom (TGIW), which Handley estimates has reached over three thousand men in the metro area since its founding, representing five hundred churches.

The same summer, in June 2000, the Servant Foundation began operating (and in 2018 changed its name to The Signatry). The

Servant Foundation was founded by business and ministry leaders who were seeking to inspire and facilitate radical biblical generosity to help ministries and advance the Great Commission. For context, in 1998 Emmitt Mitchell and I (Bill) decided to help Emmitt's brother Thurman Mitchell with an inner city ministry. Thurman was a news anchor for the local CBS affiliate, and he pastored a church in urban Kansas City. The three of us began a youth ministry for the city. As funds ran low, we realized we needed a better way to raise money than traditional fundraising. We needed to "connect the donors with the doers," as Thurman stated. Conversations began with a few like-minded local business people: Pat Lloyd, Frank Brown, Frank Mall, and Mark Bainbridge. By June 2000, the group decided to start the Servant Foundation and affiliated with the National Christian Foundation. Since its founding, the Servant Foundation, which later changed its name to The Signatry, has facilitated gifts into donor advised funds of more than $3 billion while granting out over $2 billion to ministries both locally and nationwide.

Unconventional Business Network began in 2001 as Integrity Resource Center. Its founder, Rick Boxx, had become a Christian years before. In the early 1990s, he had been running from God for decades when he was hired as a chief lending officer to help a troubled bank. The bank also brought in a new president, who happened to be a strong believer. For the first time, Boxx encountered a manager who ran the bank based on principles in Scripture. Boxx observed that the principles worked. The bank started thriving.

The influence of the bank president, combined with a near-death experience when Boxx was caught in a riptide in Hawaii, shook Boxx up. He decided to return to God. After Boxx returned to church, he started wondering if anyone besides the bank president was teaching these principles. He found Larry Burkett's ministry, Crown Financial Ministries, and became a trained counselor with them. In 1995, Boxx sold the small community bank he was running and started praying about what to do next. He felt God telling him, "You keep asking, 'Why isn't anyone teaching these principles to business leaders?' That's what you need to do."

> "You keep asking, 'Why isn't anyone teaching these principles . . .?' That's what you need to do."

Boxx started his own consulting company to help businesses put together business plans based on biblical principles from the book of Nehemiah. Crown Financial Ministries had many business owners call in on their radio show about crisis situations, and the ministry asked Boxx if they could start referring businesses in crisis over to his consulting company. At the height of Crown Financial's radio show, Boxx was helping over six hundred businesses a year. The consulting kept growing and branched out into books, curriculum, and counseling.

In 2001, Boxx says his "board woke up." They realized that God was doing incredible things, and the business looked more like a ministry than a consulting company. They switched to a nonprofit model and started Integrity Resource Center, which later changed its name in 2018 to Unconventional Business Network. Over the past two decades, the ministry has helped businesses discover biblical principles for management both locally and nationwide.

Churches Unite in Prayer

Meanwhile, the Citywide Prayer Movement continued to increase the unity among churches in the Kansas City area. Around 2004, Gary Schmitz took over the movement and formed a board. The Citywide Prayer Movement was a mixture of inner-city churches and suburban churches, African American pastors and white pastors. Boxx was invited to join the movement. He recalls that in the early days, the group met every Friday morning and spent three to four hours praying and getting to know each other. As they deepened relationships with each other, cultural and denominational barriers were knocked down.

The movement swelled in numbers over the years. The group transformed into what they called "Village Fires," where clusters of pastors gathered locally each month to pray for the community. Under the leadership of Gary Schmitz, a dozen Village Fires formed, with each group representing leaders from up to fifteen churches. The movement took off and kept growing until in 2012 they decided they were ready to do more. It was time to put their prayers into action. It was time for churches to step up and impact the city.

They formed a group called Elevate KC to serve the city as churches united. They talked to city leaders and decided there were four major issues in Kansas City that needed to be addressed, and they formed four task forces in Kansas City to tackle the following problems:

1. Fatherlessness
2. Human trafficking
3. Education
4. Racial reconciliation

Thirty organizations throughout Kansas City signed a covenant with each other, promising that they would pull in their spheres of influence to begin tackling these problems. Each of these organizations represented hundreds of churches. Once Elevate KC formed the task forces, they began surveying what had already been done regarding each issue, and they brainstormed new ways to work together and influence the city.

Fatherlessness

This issue is pervasive. The US Census Bureau estimates that 33 percent of children do not live with their biological father. Moreover, a study by City-Data.com ranked 101 cities in the United States with the highest population of single-parent households. Kansas City, Kansas, placed on the list at number 72, with a listing of 56 percent of households as single-parent, assumedly many of them without a father.

Fatherlessness also includes foster children, today's orphans in America. The Global Orphan Project joined the fatherlessness task force. Begun in 2004 by Kansas Citians Mike and Beth Fox, the Global Orphan Project had been working with orphans worldwide and increased their involvement in partnering with Kansas City's churches. They developed software to serve needs of foster children quickly and effectively once children were removed from their birth homes. The Global Orphan Project, as part of the task force, worked with churches to train them in using the software to help children in need.

Human Trafficking

Fatherlessness fuels human trafficking, both in Kansas City and across the nation. According to a 2009 study by Williamson and Prior, "77 percent of women in prostitution had either been in foster care or had some level of contact with child protective services." Boxx recalls how once the human trafficking task force was formed, it began to take on a life of its own, uniting many anti-trafficking agencies around Kansas City such as KC Street Hope, Restoration House, Exodus Cry, Veronica's Voice, and many others. The group meets regularly to strategize on combating human trafficking.

Annually during the years 2013 to 2016, abolitionists from around the nation gathered for a weekend Abolition Summit hosted in Kansas City to learn more about how to fight human trafficking.

Education

Perhaps the most striking result of the Citywide Prayer Movement came through the development of Caring for Kids, a nonprofit to connect churches and businesses with local schools. In 2012, a Village Fire group was meeting every week to pray for the city and for the schools. They had no preconceived notions of how to pray or what to pray for; they just met regularly to pray. Then one day, the superintendent of the Olathe School District called the leaders of the Village Fire and asked to meet with them. He had been asking who had the most contact with pastors in Olathe, and someone had referred him to the Citywide Prayer Movement meeting there locally.

However, at the meeting, leaders of the Olathe School District thought that Citywide Prayer had called the meeting. Citywide Prayer thought the Olathe School District had called the meeting. Neither side knew exactly why they were meeting together. While they were all gathered, one of the leaders of the prayer group asked what the school district needed from churches. Leaders from the school district shared that the Olathe School District was commonly thought of as wealthy because it was located in Johnson County. However, 450 homeless families lived in the district, and they had more needs than the city knew how to handle. The school district needed churches to step up and fill in the gap.

> *They needed churches to step up and fill in the gap.*

The prayer group got to work. They developed a simple model: for each school, two churches and one business would come together and adopt the school. They sent the kids from low-income families home with backpacks of food for the weekend and provided school supplies at the beginning of the year. Within eighteen months, every school in the Olathe School District had been adopted by churches and businesses. Eventually, the program became the nonprofit Caring for Kids. They now serve the school districts of Kansas City, Kansas; Kansas City, Missouri; Olathe; Shawnee Mission; Raytown; Hickman Mills; Center; and Grandview.

Racial Reconciliation

The fourth area of focus for Elevate KC was racial reconciliation. In examining the need for racial reconciliation in Kansas City, it's vital to look at it in relation to the other three issues.

Regarding the issue of fatherlessness, a black child is about three times more likely to have grown up without a father than a white child, according to the National Center for Fathering. According to a 2012 report from the US Census Bureau, at least half of black children live in a single-parent home. In comparison, one-third of Hispanic children live in single-parent homes, and one-fifth of white children. The Missouri Department of Social Services reports that in the counties of Jackson, Clay, and Platte, black children are two to three times more likely to end up in foster care than white children.

A Caring for Kids volunteer paints a classroom for Truman Elementary in Kansas City, Missouri.

A volunteer helps students glue craft projects at Frances Willard Elementary's summer camp in partnership with Vida Abundante Church in Kansas City, Kansas.

Racial disparity also exists in victims of human trafficking. According to a master's thesis by Alison Philips in 2017, the overall demographic of the Kansas City metro area is 74 percent white and 12.5 percent black. However, adult human trafficking victims do not match the ratios. Trafficking victims are only 54 percent white and 43 percent black.

There is a similar racial disparity in education. Comparing school districts' demographics and graduation rates, one can see that the predominantly black Kansas City, Missouri, School District has a graduation rate of 65.3 percent. In contrast, the predominantly white Blue Valley School District has a graduation rate of 94.7 percent. A student from the Blue Valley School District is almost twice as likely to graduate than a student from Kansas City School District. Across the board, whatever the issue, the black community is at a disadvantage.

Boxx shared in an interview that more honest conversations have been happening between suburban and urban pastors since the racial reconciliation initiative began. In the meetings, Boxx heard pastors from the African American community express how frustrating it was to hear white church leaders saying, "We want to help," but when there was a shooting in a black neighborhood, those same church leaders were nowhere to be found.

Though these honest conversations are just the beginning of bringing about change, they are a step in the right direction. Greg Ealey, a pastor of Colonial Presbyterian Church and executive director of Elevate KC, shared in an interview how encouraged he was at church unity in Kansas City. "When I travel the nation, I find that most cities are trying to do what we are doing and often ask us for help to get them started," said Ealey. "The church of Kansas City has come a long way. We had a rough start, and we still have work to do, but there is much to be celebrated."

Uniting for the City

As the Citywide Prayer Movement continued to grow through local Village Fire prayer meetings, they decided to unite with a network called the Sending Project. Headed up by Eric Rochester, the Sending Project aims to "build missional awareness, community, and collaboration among a diversity of churches." At a Sending Project banquet in 2017, Rochester shared their goal of increasing the number of people praying in Kansas City by mobilizing one hundred thousand in prayer.

> "The church of Kansas City has come a long way. We had a rough start, and we still have work to do, but there is much to be celebrated."
>
> -Greg Ealey

Former pastor Gary Kendall attended the banquet. He and his wife Belinda were pastoring Indian Creek Community Church in Olathe. During the banquet, Gary Kendall felt God highlighting the prayer project and calling him to work toward fulfilling that goal. After confirmation from others in the Sending Project and Citywide Prayer, along with encouragement from their church, the Kendalls turned their church leadership over to another couple and ventured into God's calling to serve the citywide church in Kansas City. Gary Kendall formed a new ministry called Love KC, a partnership between Citywide Prayer Movement and the Sending Project.

Their goal was to raise up and equip one or more disciples living on mission in every neighborhood in Kansas City. There were four hundred neighborhoods in the Kansas City metro area (defining neighborhoods by local public grade school boundaries).

"The prayer was that no one would wake up in Kansas City who wasn't being prayed for by their family name, cared for as the Spirit leads, and shared with by a disciple of Jesus," according to Kendall.

Love KC offered an opportunity for anyone to sign up online, submit their address, and receive a daily email from an online database of five neighbors to pray for each day. "Within one year, half of the neighborhoods within the thirty-mile radius of Kansas City had a person claiming their neighborhood for Jesus," Kendall said. "Over sixteen hundred praying disciples signed up in 2017 alone."

Over the past two decades, throughout Kansas City many new ministries began as church leaders came together to pray for their city. Movements like Citywide Prayer, Elevate KC, the Sending Project, and Love KC have brought the church together around social justice and prayer. Gatherings such as What If the Church and Concerned Clergy Coalition provide platforms for partnerships and service throughout the city. What If the Church has brought together ninety churches who work together for the city. The Concerned Clergy Coalition was originally founded by Dr. Wallace S. Hartfield Sr., pastor of Metropolitan Missionary Baptist Church for forty years. The Concerned Clergy Coalition is currently led by Pastor Cassandra Wainwright. The coalition is made up of pastors primarily in the urban core and focuses on "the discussion and resolution of many community problems in Kansas City's urban core since its creation."

Throughout the city, churches are banding together in partnerships to more effectively impact their communities. As Ealey stated, though much remains to be done, "there is much to be celebrated."

Grains of Sand

Modern history is the most daunting history to write because, every day, it is still being written. Choosing ministries to highlight in this chapter felt like choosing grains of sand from a beach or drops of water from the ocean. No particle is more important than the next. Each one is necessary to comprise the whole. We recognize that although we have told the stories of a few ministries and churches, we have left out the majority. Yet whether mentioned in this book or not, each church and ministry plays a vital role in Kansas City.

We can relate to the Apostle John as he writes the story of Jesus. He reaches the end of his account and writes, "Jesus did many other things as well. If every one of them were written down, I suppose that even the whole world would not have room for the books that would be written" (John 21:25, NIV). In Jesus's life on earth, He accomplished far more than could possibly be recorded.

But as we look to the future of what God is doing in our community and what He will do, we remain hopeful, optimistic, and encouraged. We see the church in Kansas City, while not perfect, working together. Anecdotally, as we interface with leaders from other cities, they tell us that they sense the same thing we do: God is on the move in our city. Churches and ministries are working together for the good of our city. This kind of activity is not true of every city.

We know we are not perfect. There are battles ahead, but we've faced them in the past, and we know the church of Kansas City will remain vibrant and strong. Our hope is that the few stories we've written here will encourage you to see how God has been at work in our city. But even more, we hope these stories will encourage you to engage right where you are—like so many of the saints before. Do what you can. Be faithful. Pray.

It's with eager anticipation that we wait to see how the next chapters will unfold. But we are sure they'll be great ones.

Epilogue

EPILOGUE

We've taken you on a grand journey—from the earliest days of Kansas City to the present. As you've read this history on the spiritual roots of our city, we hope that you've picked up on the theme: God has been present from the very beginning. But there are so many key themes:

1. The river was central to the early life of the city; the river brought the good and the bad.
2. The river also brought great diversity. Even today, we see diversity in our city reflected in the vast number of churches of every kind.
3. The first church was established with a gift from a businessman, Francois Choteau.
4. The city was always a missional city—an area where missionaries came to make the gospel of Jesus Christ known—as witnessed by the number of missions established.
5. By the 1830s, the land around the river was valuable enough that it was subject to a fraudulent action by James McGee. But the auction was overturned through the efforts of a man named John Calvin McCoy.
6. The flood of 1844 nearly wiped out the city but rerouted the river such that Kansas City became the dominant riverboat landing site instead of Independence.

The hard work in establishing a city is equal to those who shaped it further—like the artist sculpting a great work of art. The shapers of our city are many:

1. Not only was there John Calvin McCoy, but some of the early church planters—Thomas James, Dr. Nathan Scarritt, and John Wornall. Some might only recognize these names as city landmarks, or perhaps not at all, but their work cannot be ignored.
2. Sarah and Kersey Coates were among those who fought valiantly against slavery, and after the Civil War, Kansas City was home to very vibrant African American churches.

3. Dreamers like Mrs. T. C. Cox and Rev. Dr. Henry Hopkins believed Kansas City would become a City Beautiful and the church would be unified. Hopkins inspired August Meyer to drive the establishment of Kansas City's extensive park system.
4. City leaders worked together to bring the famed evangelist Dwight L. Moody to our city in 1899.
5. Have you heard of Longview Farm? Longview Lake? Or perhaps Liberty Memorial? All were part of the efforts of a strong believer in Christ, R. A. Long.

We could go on and on. What about William Volker, Simeon Armour, Adriance Van Brunt, Robert Gillham, William T. Campbell, David and Beulah Bulkley, Fred Olander Sr., Rev. William H. Thomas, Rev. Lawrence Scott, Esther Brown, Rev. Robert Meneilly, Al and Vidy Metsker, Ted Nissen, Marilyn Griffin, and Gary Schmitz? These are but a few, let alone the thousands upon thousands who labored tirelessly for the good of the church in Kansas City. They are part of the "hall of fame of faith" in Kansas City.

Throughout Kansas City's history, there's been good and bad. The same era that brought the mob rule of Tom Pendergast also brought Napoleon Dible and the nation's largest men's Bible study. The prostitution house of Annie Chambers collided with the work of the City Union Mission and ultimately led to her conversion to faith. A Jewish leader, Rabbi Samuel Mayerberg, at his own peril spoke out against the Pendergast machine and ultimately helped bring down the crime machine. Racial unrest has been a long-standing issue at which the church has been front and center.

In many respects, Kansas City has followed the trajectory of the nation. Strong faith and strong leaders marked the early and formative years of the city. But as the strength of our nation's faith dwindled, so did the faith of our city. However, it seems we've been granted resurgence with efforts like the Citywide Prayer Movement. Its covering of prayer has given rise to the birth of new ministries—from missions, to businesses, to pastors, to accountability, to generosity.

These themes of church, business, problems, prayer and concerted action tell us some of the formula for success in the future. The problems we face currently are real, and some may seem daunting. But the dream for our city as a place of flourishing—a city beautiful—remains unchanged. As we look to the past, we can learn and gain hope that the future remains bright.

    We invite you to join with your local church, some of the organizations mentioned in the previous chapter and be part of writing the story of Kansas City for the coming decades.

God's Plan for Cities:

Agents of Change, Forces for Good

Mike King, director of Youthfront, states that in ancient times, saints were tied to cities, such as St. Francis of Assisi, Benedict of Nursia, Augustine of Hippo, and the Cappadocian fathers. Even Martin Luther was connected to Wittenberg, and John Calvin to Geneva. They were all connected to a specific place. "It takes years to really prepare the field, fertilize, and cultivate the land before good things really start to emerge forth," King says.

Cities are part of our identity and of our calling. Timothy Keller, pastor of an inner-city congregation in New York City, interprets why God created cities in his article, "A Theology of Cities." According to Keller, God created cities for our good. There are three main reasons God created cities: to protect the vulnerable, to foster creativity, and to reveal God.

Protect the Vulnerable

The city offers protection for society. Instead of being out on our own, we have the safe haven of each other. Back in the Bible, God created "cities of refuge." If someone accidentally killed another, the accused could flee to a city of refuge and find shelter. In early days, this meant cities with walls. Now it means the protection of a denser population. Keller observes, "Even today, people like the homeless, or new immigrants, or the poor, or people with 'deviant' lifestyles, must live in the city." The increased population of cities allows minority groups to band together and protect each other. Ironically, "it is hard for middle-class families to live in cities, [b]ut for anyone who is not part of the dominant culture (singles, the poor, ethnic minorities, etc.) the city has great advantages over non-urban areas." The city seems hostile to dominant groups, but to minorities, it offers protection.

Unfortunately, this feature also offers protection for evil. Because the city is a center of diversity in race, culture, and thought, it also produces conflict and strife. And because of their intrinsic higher population density, cities allow people of evil intent to come and find refuge in banding together. Whereas a criminal might be on his own in a small town, he or she can find ready company in a city.

Foster Creativity

The nature of cities draws talents together. People can be more productive in large numbers. Creative types live in close proximity competing with each other, building off of each other's ideas, spurring each other on to bigger and better accomplishments. This first happened in Babel, according to the biblical account listed in Genesis 11. The people of Babel wanted to make a name for themselves and started building a magnificent tower. However, God saw that if they were all working together in unity, they could accomplish anything, so He created different languages and scattered them. The scattering put a stop to their creativity.

When people gather, their efforts inspire each other, making cities the hub of culture. Inspiration shoots as high as the skyscrapers when multiple businesses compete for the same customers. Cities force everyone in them to create harder and better. They birth creativity. The bad side of this creativity, Keller points out, is that this self-actualization can lead to self-idolization. People come to the city to "make it big." Just like the people at Babel, they gather in the city and say, "Come, let us build ourselves a city . . . so that we may make a name for ourselves..." (Genesis 11:4, NIV). They want to become great. In doing so, life becomes all about them.

Reveal God

Third, cities are a place to meet God. Cities have always been the center of new ideas and the birthplace of new cultures. According to Keller's "A Theology of Cities," cities are where Christianity first spread. In the Apostle Paul's missionary journeys, he went from city to city, letting the new ideas about God take root. The close proximity of people proved to be the perfect soil in which the teachings of Jesus's followers could take root, and the Gospel quickly spread, sending out its shoots along trade routes and springing up in new cities, until it had grown into a giant tree within the Roman Empire. As a result, by 300 AD, 50 percent of the urban populations of the empire were Christian, while over 90 percent of the countryside was still pagan. In fact, the word "pagan," now synonymous with "godless," has its root from the word "paganus," meaning "farmer" or "man of the country."

The beauty of cities, according to Keller, is that you're exposed to new ideas when you're in the city. You're challenged by beliefs that are different from your own and that are held by people better than yourself. You'll be forced either to discard your old ideas or to become more strongly attached to them than ever before. You're stretched and challenged in new ways. Cities force you to decide what you believe.

Paul went first to the cities because he knew that cities are the birthplaces of cultural thought. We can't know God apart from His revelation through people. God has left the knowledge of Himself—the Bible—in the hands of people. It's only through Bible translators, pastors, books, sermons, and the help of people that we learn about God. Thus it makes sense that His religion first spread through cities, the hubs of society.

Cities Happen by Choice

Cities don't just magically appear. They evolve from ordinary people like you and me. Every highway, every park, every skyscraper was first a dream. Then a developer found an investor to fund it, an architect to design it, and a construction crew to build it. Today, we drive through Kansas City and see rows of brick buildings silhouetted by skyscrapers. But we often don't see the hard work it took to create them. We forget the people who went before us—those who envisioned what the city would become—but we reap the benefits of their choices.

The same is true of the church. The church as a whole in Kansas City exists because of thousands of people's choices over hundreds of years. The Chouteau family came in with the French fur traders and started the first church in Kansas City. The city's founding fathers, Baptist minister Isaac McCoy and his son John Calvin McCoy, came to Kansas City as missionaries and then founded the city. As the city grew, in neighborhoods where there was no church, citizens trekked through the mud of new housing developments to their neighbors' houses, building prayer meetings and Bible studies from scratch. Their names have become memorialized on schools, roads, and counties—all paying homage to the choices they made.

Once the church was formed, church leaders fought crime, spoke against injustice, and inspired their congregations. Through stories of Rabbi Mayerberg who ended Kansas City's mob era, Esther Brown who pushed Kansas schools to integrate, Rev. David Bulkley who started City Union Mission, and many other individuals who brought about societal change in Kansas City, you've seen that we can make a difference. Whether famous or anonymous, those who did the hard work and pulled people together were the ones who changed history.

Both the city and the church are what we, as individuals working collectively, choose to make it. Our home is our choice. When we look at societal patterns, it's easy to feel helpless. We're like fish swimming upstream. How can we possibly change the current of the river? By ourselves, we're individual fish that can't change the course of a river. But we hope you've seen through this book that together we can be the flood force that completely re-charts the course of a river and forever changes history.

Cities are Under God's Sovereignty

Cities are the result of our choices. Cities are also under God's sovereignty. Proverbs 16:9 states, "In their hearts humans plan their course, but the LORD establishes their steps." The Missouri River itself has proved God's sovereignty that divinely directs human choices. A fateful flood in 1844, a few years after the Town of Kansas was formed, changed an entire city's destiny. Before the flood, the town was a tiny trading post next door to the booming town of Independence, the main launching point for pioneers as they ventured into the west. However, the flood changed the course of the Missouri River and made Westport the more strategic landing. Thus commerce was built around what later became Kansas City, and Independence became just a neighboring town. From that fateful flood in 1844 to the West Bottoms' flood one hundred years later that flooded the meatpacking factories and ended Kansas City's days as a cattle town, God has been using outside forces to divinely direct the city. Our times are in God's hands (Psalm 31:15), and our lives are at His mercy. It is this divine dance with God, faith's classic struggle of who is in charge, that keeps us always striving to better our city and yet always looking to the hand of God to guide us—and wondering what He will do next.

Timeline
Small Group Discussion Guide

Chapter 1
Fur Traders and Missionaries

Several of Kansas City's first settlers came as missionaries to the area. Driven by compassion for those who had been displaced by the government, they came to spread the gospel of Jesus and serve the oppressed.

Focus passage: Hebrews 13:1-3

1. According to the passage, what role should the church play in addressing social issues?

. . . .
. . . .
. . . .

2. Under the Indian Removal Act of 1830, the American Indians were forced to leave their lands, and many of them died as a result. How did Rev. Isaac McCoy and Rev. Thomas Johnson "remember those who are mistreated"? What did they sacrifice in order to do so?

. . . .
. . . .
. . . .

3.. Do we see people groups or certain demographics today who are caught on the hard side of a government decision?

. . . .
. . . .
. . . .

4. Sometimes we feel sorry for people caught under injustice but also feel separated from them. They're too far away or too different from us, and reaching them would be too inconvenient. What are some ways we can bridge the gap?

. . . .
. . . .
. . . .

5. Looking at your examples listed under Question 3, what creative steps can Christians today take to comfort or defend people caught in injustice?

. . . .
. . . .
. . . .

For Further Reflection
Defending the oppressed: Proverbs 31:8-9; Isaiah 58:6-9; Hebrews 11:24-27.

Chapter 2
A Faulty Auction and a Flood

When a flood wiped out the small Town of Kansas, the town seemed ruined forever. However, the flood uncovered the rock landing which changed the small town into the Kansas City we know today.

Isn't that how life often is? Surprises come. We plan, we build, and then life happens. At the time, the trials seem insurmountable, but later we can look back and see God's divine intervention.

Focus passage: 1 Corinthians 3:6-7

1. These verses refer to the growth of believers. How could they also relate to the growth of a city?

. . . .
. . . .
. . . .

2. Kansas City would have been the Independence metro area, save for the flood of 1844. The flood changed the river, but it took an entrepreneur to see how the change could profit the town. In 1 Corinthians 3:6-7, Paul recognizes this mysterious relationship between our work and God's divine control. In what ways have you seen God's provision interacting with your own decisions?

. . . .
. . . .
. . . .

3. What are some examples from your own life of trials or inconveniences that turned out to be God's divine provision?

. . . .
. . . .
. . . .

4. John Calvin McCoy was called the "Father of Kansas City," and Berenice Chouteau the "Grand Dame" of Kansas City. They were both famous as leaders in the city, but first came their sacrificial service for the city. In what ways did they "plant" and "water" Kansas City?

. . . .
. . . .
. . . .

5. Both Isaac McCoy and John Calvin McCoy made sacrifices to serve the poor. Isaac travelled to D.C. nine times to defend Native Americans' right to land, and John Calvin gave up his horse and supplies to John Sutter. The son's sacrifice brought in millions of dollars in revenue for the city, while the father's sacrifices never effected permanent change in D.C. Was one sacrifice better than the other? How do we judge which causes are worthy of sacrifice?

. . . .
. . . .
. . . .

6. Where do you see this same spirit of service in leaders today?

. . . .
. . . .
. . . .

For Further Reflection
Sacrifice in serving others: Luke 6:38; Acts 20:24, 35; Philippians 2:17; Mark 8:34-35

Chapter 3
The Civil War Splits the Church

The issues of the Civil War severed Reverend Jonathan B. Fuller's congregation so deeply that they split a year after the war had officially ended.

Throughout church history, churches have split over countless issues. As we move forward, we must look at history to determine when it is wise to split and when we must fight for unity.

Focus passage: Romans 14:1-4 & 14:19

1. According to the above passage, how should we treat those in the church who believe differently than we do?

. . . .
. . . .
. . . .

2. Read 1 Corinthians 6:11-13 and 11:17-19. What do these passages tell us about division in the church? How does this relate to the passage in Romans?

. . . .
. . . .
. . . .

3. In some passages, Christians are instructed to give each other freedom and not judge each other, while in other passages they are instructed to pull away from disobedient believers. How do we determine when to make a moral judgment and when to give freedom for someone's conscience to differ from our own?

. . . .
. . . .
. . . .

4. When is division necessary in the church? How does a leader determine when to fight for unity and when to break away?

. . . .
. . . .
. . . .

5. Based on the above passages, do you agree or disagree with Fuller's decision to pull away and form a separate church? Why or why not?

. . . .
. . . .
. . . .

For Further Reflection

Maintaining unity versus separating: John 17:20-23; Acts 15:36-40; 2 Corinthians 6:14-7:1; Philippians 2:2; Philippians 4:2

Chapter 4
Growth through Diversity

During the late 1800s, many new immigrants came to Kansas City, whether as refugees or as workers looking for a fresh start. Every immigration requires a certain measure of faith. New beginnings always precipitate an adventure into the unknown.

Like the Exodusters and immigrants, faith often travels in groups. As we join together, we strengthen each other's faith.

Focus passage: Hebrews 11:8-9

1. When a reporter asked the Exodusters what their plan was, a woman replied, "The good Lord will see us safe through." How was the Exoduster's faith similar to Abraham's?

. . . .
. . . .
. . . .

2. Tell about a time you followed God in faith, not knowing the outcome. What was the result?

. . . .
. . . .
. . . .

3. The Armour family left a legacy of faith by serving the Exodusters, and this wasn't the first time they served the city. In what other ways did the Armours leave a legacy?

. . . .
. . . .
. . . .

DISCOVERING THE PAST TO SHAPE OUR FUTURE

4. How do families influence each other to live out their faith?

. . . .
. . . .
. . . .

5. Read Hebrews 10:24. What can you do to encourage your family in their faith?

. . . .
. . . .
. . . .

For Further Reflection
Faith in God's provision: Deuteronomy 1:29-33; Deuteronomy 2:7; Psalm 48:14; Matthew 6:25-34

Chapter 5
Dreamers Build the City

Our spiritual well-being and our cities' physical well-being are inextricably linked. Through his preaching, Dr. Hopkins inspired an entire city to greater heights. Robert Long and other city leaders followed his example by building the Convention Hall and the Liberty Memorial. They put their faith into action by serving the city.

Focus passage: Ezekiel 36:33-36

1. In these verses, what does God promise the cities of Israel?

. . . .
. . . .
. . . .

2. What do these promises reveal about God's heart for cities?

. . . .
. . . .
. . . .

3. Read Exodus 31:1-5. The first person in the Bible to be filled with the Spirit was Bezalel, a craftsman. God gave him creativity and skill for directing the construction of the tabernacle. Why would God care about the quality of the tabernacle's design and construction?

. . . .
. . . .
. . . .

4. How does this relate to God's design for cities?

. . . .
. . . .
. . . .

5. As a minister, Rev. Hopkins put great effort into inspiring his congregation to beautify the city. In light of the discussion from the previous questions, is it the church's role to make the city beautiful? Why or why not?

. . . .
. . . .
. . . .

For Further Reflection
Caring for the city: Genesis 1:26, 2:15; Jeremiah 29:7; Hebrews 11:10; Revelation 21:1-2

Chapter 6
Mobsters and Madams

Law and grace. These two elements often get pitted against each other, as if they cannot possibly coexist. Yet both are necessary for a healthy society.

Focus passage: Romans 8:3-4

1. Dr. Martin Luther King Jr. once said, "It may be true that the law cannot change the heart, but it can restrain the heartless." What role does law play in society?

. . . .
. . . .
. . . .

2. The Church Federation (later renamed the Society for Suppression of Commercialized Vice) worked hard to change Kansas City's laws regarding prostitution and other social evils. Was the Church Federation in Kansas City successful in fulfilling this role? Why or why not?

. . . .
. . . .
. . . .

3. Read Romans 8:3. The Bulkleys chose compassion instead of legislation as a way to help the city. Instead of judging the poor and marginalized, they moved into their neighborhood. How did their choice exemplify Romans 8:3?

. . . .
. . . .
. . . .

4. How was the city changed by their choice?

....
....
....

5. Rabbi Mayerberg said, "It is the responsibility of the minister to lead in the movement to eradicate such evil powers." Do you agree with his statement? Why or why not?

....
....
....

6. What is the relationship between fighting for legal reform and recognizing that only Jesus can change people's hearts?

....
....
....

For Further Reflection:
Grace and forgiveness: Isaiah 43:25, Daniel 9:9, Micah 7:18-19, Acts 3:19, Ephesians 2:4-5

Chapter 7
Seeds of Change

When facing difficult history, we must feel the weight. Galatians 6 says "each one should carry his own load." Yet the same chapter also says, "Carry each other's burdens." We are each responsible to pull our own weight, but when we see someone with a burden too heavy to carry, we pick it up and carry it with them.

Focus passage: Nehemiah 1:3-7

1. Nehemiah prays this prayer 141 years after the fall of Jerusalem. He could not possibly have shared personally in the sin that led to the city's downfall. Yet he prays, "[W]e have sinned against you. Even I and my father's house have sinned." Why did Nehemiah view Israel's historic sin as his own responsibility?

. . . .
. . . .
. . . .

2. What could some of the benefits of historic repentance be? What would the drawbacks be?

. . . .
. . . .
. . . .

3. Do you agree or disagree with the concept of repenting for ancestors' historic sin? Why or why not?

. . . .
. . . .
. . . .

4. Read Deuteronomy 15:12-15. When a Hebrew slave was released after working for six years, God wanted the slaveholder to equip the slave from the slaveholder's flock, threshing floor, and winepress. This meant that every freed slave immediately had food and a source of income. They could be financially independent from the start. Why do you think God gave this command?

....
....
....

5. Was this done for the slave in America? What were the consequences?

....
....
....

6. Abraham Lincoln issued the Emancipation Proclamation in 1863, over 150 years ago. Systematic oppression of African Americans occurred for the next 100 years, until the civil rights movement took place about 50 years ago. How do these historic events continue to shape the present?

....
....
....

For Further Reflection:
Repentance: Daniel 9:4-19, Acts 3:19-20, James 5:16

Chapter 8
Taking Back the Youth

If you trace the genealogy of the stories of the Jesus movement, you can track a spiritual genealogy similar to Paul and Timothy's. The lineage started in the 1940s with Henrietta Mears's Sunday school class. She discipled Bill Bright, who founded Campus Crusade for Christ (which became Cru). He discipled Ted Nissen, who pastored Colonial Presbyterian Church. The links continued up to Mike Bickle, who founded the International House of Prayer of Kansas City. And the chain continues today.

This story is merely one example of thousands of lives changed during the Jesus movement, and we can still see the effects years later.

Focus passage: Acts 4:12-21

1. Why were Peter and John unstoppable?

. . . .
. . . .
. . . .

2. After reading this chapter, what do you think caused the Jesus movement?

. . . .
. . . .
. . . .

3. Could another movement like it happen again today? Why or why not?

. . . .
. . . .
. . . .

4. The stories from the Jesus movement were about the crazy Christians, the ones obsessed with Jesus. Christians met with other Christians every day. They talked about Jesus with everyone they knew. They skipped class. They spent all day praying. It's easy to look at the stories shared and think, "That's too extreme," or "That's not for me." But what was the fruit of being "extreme," "crazy," and "obsessed"?

. . . .
. . . .
. . . .

5. Is their radical faith worth imitating today? If so, how would our lives have to change?

. . . .
. . . .
. . . .

6. The summer Ichthus program at Colonial saw so much success that they boiled down their strategy to five essential elements that other churches could replicate: (1) ministry is relational, (2) devotion is the top priority of a disciple, (3) community adorns the gospel, (4) Jesus' strategy is discipleship, and (5) salvation is a free gift. How do you see these themes implemented in your own church community?

. . . .
. . . .
. . . .

For Further Reflection
Discipleship: Matthew 28:18-20; 1 Corinthians 4:15-17; Philippians 3:17; 2 Timothy 2:2; Hebrews 13:7.

Chapter 9
Freedom Marches and Riots

The Metropolitan Inter-Church Agency had established a reputation as being capable of serving the city. When a crisis occurred, the church was the first place city leaders looked to for help.

Focus passage: Matthew 5:13-16

1. What does it mean to be the salt of the earth and the light of the world?

. . . .
. . . .
. . . .

2. How did the city know it could depend on the church?

. . . .
. . . .
. . . .

3. Read Psalm 122:6-9. What does the psalmist's attitude toward Jerusalem show us about the role between the church and the city?

. . . .
. . . .
. . . .

4. If there were a crisis in our city today, do you think city leaders would call on the church for help? Why or why not?

. . . .
. . . .
. . . .

5. What can be done to maintain/increase trust between the city and the church?

....
....
....

For Further Reflection

Pursuing peace: Matthew 5:9; 2 Corinthians 13:11; James 3:18

Chapter 10
A New Millennium of Growth

It seems that whenever people accomplish great tasks, they do so in groups—John Adams and Thomas Jefferson; Thomas Edison and Henry Ford; C. S. Lewis and J. R. R. Tolkien. We are better together, and God knows this. That's why He always encourages us toward unity.

Focus passage: Ephesians 4:3-6

1. What other famous friendships can you think of, either from history or the present? How do our friendships influence our productivity?

. . . .
. . . .
. . . .

2. In our focus passage, Paul encourages Christians to "keep the unity of the Spirit through the bond of peace." Why?

. . . .
. . . .
. . . .

3. During the turn of the millennium, church leaders began collaborating in new ways to serve the city. In what ways did they exemplify this verse?

. . . .
. . . .
. . . .

4. Read John 17:21. What is Jesus's prayer for believers? Why would He pray this?

....
....
....

5. What is the value of being united with believers?

....
....
....

6. How do we accomplish unity?

....
....
....

7. As Pastor Greg Ealey stated, "The church of Kansas City has come a long way. We had a rough start, and we still have work to do, but there is much to be celebrated." Considering everything you've read in this book, what areas of church life can we celebrate—historic and modern day, both in your church and in churches across Kansas City?

....
....
....

For Further Reflection
Unity: Romans 12:4-5; 1 Corinthians 1:10; Ephesians 2:21-22; Philippians 2:1-2.

God's Plan for Cities: Agents of Change, Forces for Good

Cities are part of God's perfect creation. As with any aspect of creation, they can be used for good or misused for evil. The passage below reflects God's purpose for cities.

Focus passage: Psalm 107:4-9

1. What do you think of when you think of cities?

....
....
....

2. According to the passage, what was the peoples' need, and how did God fill it?

....
....
....

3. What role did the city play in God's rescue? (See vv. 4 and 7.)

....
....
....

4. What does this passage show us about God's purpose for cities?

....
....
....

5. Read Jonah 4:11. When we look at cities, we often see the external elements—skyscrapers, road systems, and crowds of people. When God looks at cities, what does He see? What does He feel?

....
....
....

6. Read Jeremiah 29:4-7. Tim Keller writes regarding this passage, "[H]ere the Israelites are in exile, conquered by this wicked, terrible nation called Babylon. What does he say to them? He says, 'Identify with the prosperity of that city.' He does not say, 'Go into the streets and preach to the city. Hand out tracts in the city. Then, get out.' He says, 'Settle down. Build houses. Have children. Identify with the city. Identify with the people of the city, with the well-being of the city. Weave yourselves into the city in a way that weaves wholeness and health into the city.'" According to this passage, in what ways should believers identify with the city?

....
....
....

For Further Reflection
God's purpose for cities: Genesis 11:4, Luke 13:34, Revelation 21:9-11, 22-27

Timeline
Events in Kansas City's Church History

Timeline - Events in Kansas City's Church History

Date	People Involved	Key Event	Implication for the City
Early 1800	Pioneer Priests	Minister to French Catholic fur traders	Christianity introduced to KC area
1820	Christian Missionaries	Arrive in KC to minister to Native Americans	Native Americans of KC became Christians
1830	Thomas Johnson	Establishes a Methodist Mission to the Shawnee (Shawnee Mission)	The Methodist Faith introduced to KC area
1831	Isaac McCoy, Johnston Lykins	Establish Baptist Missions to Native American tribes	The Baptist faith introduced to KC area
1831	Joseph Smith	Dedicated the temple site in Independence, Missouri	The Mormon faith introduced to KC area
1833	Francois and Berenice Chouteau	Donate money for building a small log cabin parish, dubbed "Chouteau's Church"	The first church in KC is built
1833	John Calvin McCoy	Establishes Westport	Son of Baptist missionary establishes major area of KC
1837	Society of Friends	Mission established near Merriam, Kansas	Quaker Faith introduced to KC area
1855	R. S. Thomas	Establishes First Baptist Church of Kansas City	Baptist faith now meeting in KC area

DISCOVERING THE PAST TO SHAPE OUR FUTURE

Timeline - Events in Kansas City's Church History

Date	People Involved	Key Event	Implication for the City
1863	Reverend Clark Moore	Stragglers Camp revival meetings provide a place for black Americans to worship	Second Baptist Church and Allen Chapel AME Church began
1866	Jonathan Fuller	Establishes Walnut Street Church, later known as Central Church	First Northern-sympathizing Baptist church
1875	Mennonites	Established in Kansas City	Mennonite faith introduced to Kansas City
1878	Exodusters	Thousands immigrate to Kansas City to escape the South's animosity	The African American community grows in Wyandotte County and North Kansas City, Missouri
1879	Father John Joseph Hogan	First bishop of Kansas City Diocese	KC Diocese founded
1891	R. A. Long	Long moves to Kansas City, and his lumber business becomes worth millions	Builds Longview Farm and Liberty Memorial
1897	Della Lamb	Lamb and Methodist women open a mission home to serve needy women, children, and immigrants	Church offers social services to needy families

Timeline - Events in Kansas City's Church History			
Date	People Involved	Key Event	Implication for the City
1899	D. L. Moody	Moody holds a weeklong revival in KC and preaches his last sermon there	Camp meetings and revivals became popular
1900	Second Presbyterian Church	Church burns down	Significant loss to KC congregation church
1905	Alfred Benjamin	Becomes president of United Jewish Charities	Jewish faith becomes involved in political movement
1907	Billy Sunday	Holds a revival sermon in a movie theater	KC theaters become revival sites
1908	James Sharp	Religious cult leader leads angry armed crowds	Church in KC becomes involved in politics
1910	Swedish immigrants	Settle on west side of KC	Churches are built by immigrants
1910	Italian immigrants	Settle on north side of KC	Churches are built by immigrants
1910	Russian immigrants	Settle on east side of KC	Churches are built by immigrants
1916	KC University	Established by Methodist Protestant church	KC churches become involved in education
1921	Monsignor Ernest Zechenter	Arrives in KC from Germany	Establishes St. Peter and Paul Catholic Church
1922	WOQ radio	Church service broadcasts on radio	Mormons begin broadcasting services

DISCOVERING THE PAST TO SHAPE OUR FUTURE

Timeline - Events in Kansas City's Church History

Date	People Involved	Key Event	Implication for the City
1923	David Evans, N. W. Dible	Business Men's Bible Study at First Baptist Church peaks at 52,100 men in Bible study	Churches work together for Bible study
1924	Rev. David Bulkley	Founds City Union Mission	Homeless ministry in Kansas City
1928	Rabbi Samuel S. Mayerberg	Fights Pendergast Syndicate; advocates for African Americans' rights; Founds Temple B'Nai Jehudah	Pendergast machine slows down
1935	Billy Sunday	Holds final crusade in Kansas City	KC area still active in faith
1935	Annie Chambers	Chambers donates her brothel to City Union Mission	
1943	Al and Vidy Metsker	First youth rally is held in Kansas City	Starts Youth for Christ in KC, which later becomes Youthfront
1950s	Catholic church	Catholic churches start holding biannual Kansas City youth conferences	Catholic youth have a revival; discuss issues they're facing
1952	Stonecroft	Women's ministry relocates headquarters to Kansas City	Their ministry increases in KC

Timeline - Events in Kansas City's Church History			
Date	People Involved	Key Event	Implication for the City
1956	Harold Roe Bartle	Active member of Central Presbyterian Church becomes mayor of Kansas City	City leader and active Christian for many years
1956	Don McClanen	Fellowship of Christian Athletes (FCA) relocates its headquarters from Norman, Oklahoma, to Kansas City	Students come to Christ through FCA's ministry
1962	Rev. Wallace Hartsfield Sr.	Metropolitan Missionary Baptist Church involved in nonviolent resistance	Church active in civil rights movement
1963	Ilus W. Davis	Mayor and member of Country Club Christian Church	City leader and man of faith
1967	Billy Graham	Holds KC Crusade	KC gains national exposure as a city of faith
1968	Charles Briscoe	Pastor of Paseo Baptist Church involved in peacemaking efforts after MLK's death	City leaders unite with church
1977	Zion Grove Baptist Church	Plaza floods; Zion Grove becomes headquarters for flood relief efforts	Church works with city for natural disaster relief

Timeline - Events in Kansas City's Church History			
Date	People Involved	Key Event	Implication for the City
1977	International Charismatic Conference	Baptists, Catholics, Episcopalians, Lutherans, and many other denominations gather as a statement of unity	Churches unite nationwide in KC
1978	Billy Graham	Holds second KC Crusade	City's final brothel is shut down
1987	Chris Cooper	Founds Coalition Against Pornography	Brings national exposure to KC and issue of pornography
1987	Marilyn Griffin and Ministries of New Life	First National Day of Prayer gathering in Kansas City	Beginning of Citywide Prayer Movement
1991	Emanuel Cleaver II	Prominent minister of St. James United Methodist Church becomes mayor of KC	City leader, US Representative, and man of faith
1996	Father Dennis Wait	Sanctuary of Hope is established	Prayer and retreat center for KC
1996	Promise Keepers	75,000 men attend the faith rally in KC's Arrowhead Stadium	Unity between denominations
1999	Mike Bickle	International House of Prayer of Kansas City begins	24-hour prayer and worship
1999	Jimmy and Sally Dodd	PastorServe begins	Counseling resource for pastors across the city

Timeline - Events in Kansas City's Church History				
Date	People Involved	Key Event	Implication for the City
2000	Rod Handley	Character that Counts begins	Churches focus on character, integrity, and accountability in small groups
2001	Rick Boxx	Unconventional Business Network begins	Businesses receive training on biblical principles
2004	Gary Schmitz	Encourages churches to open 24/7 Prayer Rooms	52 congregations open prayer rooms
2004	Billy Graham	Holds third crusade in KC	National exposure as city of faith

DISCOVERING THE PAST TO SHAPE OUR FUTURE

Bibliography

Books

Blair, Ed. *History of Johnson County, Kansas.* Lawrence, KS: Standard Publishing, 1915.

A Brief History of the First Congregational Church, Kansas City, Mo., 1866–1909. Edited by B. B. Seelye. Kansas City, MO: Hailman Printing, 1909.

Chapman, Rev. J. Wilbur, D.D. *The Life & Work of Dwight Lyman Moody (1837–1899).* e-book, accessed October 18, 2018, http://www.biblebelievers.com/moody/index.html. First published 1900.

Coulter, Charles E. *Take Up the Black Man's Burden: Kansas City's African American Communities 1865–1939.* Columbia, MO: University of Missouri, 2006.

Deatherage, C. P. *Early History of Greater Kansas City, Missouri and Kansas: The Prophetic City at the Mouth of the Kaw.* vol. 1. Kansas City, MO: Interstate Pub. Co., 1927.

Dodd, Monroe, and Daniel Serda. *Journeys Through Time: A Young Traveler's Guide to Kansas City History.* Kansas City, MO: Kansas City Star Books, 2000.

Donovan, Derek. *Lest the Ages Forget: Kansas City's Liberty Memorial.* Kansas City, MO: Kansas City Star Books, 2001.

Green, George Fuller. *A Condensed History of the Kansas City Area: Its Mayors and Some V.I.P.s.* Kansas City, MO: Lowell Press, 1968.

The History of Jackson County, Missouri: Containing a History of the County, Its Cities, Towns, Etc. Kansas City, MO: Union Historical Company, 1881. Reprint, Cape Girardeau, MO: Ramfre Press, 1966.

Hoggins, Olive. *Centenary History of Kansas City Churches.* Clippings from the Kansas City Journal Pages, April 1927- March 1930.

Jackson, David W. *Kansas City Chronicles: An Up-to-Date History.* Charleston, SC: History Press, 2010.

Lewis, Meriwether and William Clark. *The Journals of Lewis and Clark.* Edited by Frank Bergon. Columbia River: Penguin, 1989.

Matheny, Edward T. *Cowtown: Cattle Trails and West Bottom Tales.* Kansas City, MO: Woodneath Press, 2014.

Matthews, Bruce, Mamie Hughes, Andrew Kaplan, Christopher Leitch, Lynn Mackle, and Carol Powers. *The Kansas City Spirit: Stories of Service Above Self.* Kansas City, MO: Kansas City Star Books, 2012.

Montgomery, Rick, and Shirl Kasper. *Kansas City: An American Story.* Edited by Monroe Dodd. Kansas City, MO: Kansas City Star Books, 1999.

Morgan, Perl W. *History of Wyandotte County, Kansas, and Its People.* vol. 1. Chicago: Lewis Publishing Company, 1911.

Schirmer, Sherry Lamb. *A City Divided: The Racial Landscape of Kansas City, 1900-1960.* Columbia, MO: University of Missouri Press, 2002.

Seeing the City Through God's Eyes. Unpublished research. Contact media@thesignatry.com for a copy.

Servant Foundation: The Dream of a Generous Community. Privately published book by The Signatry, 2015. Contact media@thesignatry.com for a copy.

Shortridge, James R. *Kansas City and How It Grew, 1822-2011.* Lawrence: University Press of Kansas, 2012.

Taylor, Jimmy Bartle. *Down Home with the Chief and Miss Maggie.* Leawood, KS: Leathers Publishing, 1995.

"Through Seventy-Five Years, 1855 – 1930: A History of the First Baptist Church of Kansas City, Missouri, and Its West Side Branch." Pamphlet, First Baptist Church of Kansas City, 1930.

Whitney, Carrie Westlake. *Kansas City, Missouri: Its History and Its People, 1808–1908.* vol. 1 Chicago: S. J. Clarke Publishing, 1908.

Wilson, William H. *The City Beautiful Movement in Kansas City.* Columbia, MO: University of Missouri Press, 1964.

Woodard, W. S. *Annals of Methodism in Missouri: Containing an Outline of the Ministerial Life of More Than One Thousand Preachers, and Sketches of More Than Three Hundred. . .* Columbia, Missouri: E. W. Stephens, 1893.

News Articles

Blom, Dan. "Auction of Westwood's Youthfront Building Contents Offers Rare Opportunities." *Shawnee Mission Post*, November 13, 2013. https://shawneemissionpost.com/2013/11/13/auction-of-westwoods-youthfront-building-contents-offers-rare-opportunities-22957.

Campbell, Matt. "Billy Graham came to KC several times because the city was 'on his heart,'" *Kansas City Star*, February 21, 2018, https://www.kansascity.com/living/religion/article201421739.html.

"Doomsday Kansas City," *Kansas City Star*, July 19, 2015.

Garcia, J. Malcolm. "The Rev. David Altschul is a gift to one of the city's iconic but troubled streets," *The Pitch*, Dec. 24, 2009. https://www.pitch.com/news/article/20597601/the-rev-david-altschul-is-a-gift-to-one-of-the-citys-iconic-but-troubled-streets.

Haynes, Stephen C. and Richard D. Ralls. "Crooks Run the City," *Kansas City Star*, May 23, 1932, accessed December 3, 2018, https://www.kansascity.com/latest-news/article295362/'CROOKS-RUN-THE-CITY'.html.

Meneilly, Dr. Robert. "Dr. Meneilly . . . on Segregation," *Country Squire*, March 11, 1965.

Meneilly, Dr. Robert. "On Segregation: More from Dr. Meneilly," *Country Squire*, March 18, 1965.

Rose, Steve. "Recalling Pulpit Warnings from the Rev. Robert Meneilly on the Religious Right," *Kansas City Star*, July 12, 2014, https://www.kansascity.com/opinion/opn-columns-blogs/steve-rose/article717034.html.

Wuellner, Jean. "Audience of 42,000 Hears Billy Graham," *Kansas City Star*, September 11, 1967.

Community Interviews

Bickle, Mike (director, International House of Prayer of Kansas City). Interview with the author, June 20, 2017.

Boxx, Rick (founder and CEO, Unconventional Business Network). Interview with the author, July 6, 2017.

Bozarth, Nathaniel (anthropologist, media producer). Interview with the author, May 17, 2018.

Daughtrey, Zach (historian, Kansas City Diocese). Interview with the author, December 7, 2016.

Davies, David (gift planning advisor, Wycliffe Bible Translators). Interview with the author, June 20, 2017.

Ealey, Greg (pastor, Colonial Presbyterian Church). Email to the author, October 24, 2018.

Griffin, Marilyn (director, Ministries of New Life). Interview with the author, February 8, 2019.

Handley, Rod (founder & president, Character That Counts). Interview with the author, October 30, 2018.

Hill, Dr. Robert (former pastor, Community Christian Church). Interview with the author, June 23, 2017.

Kendall, Gary (director, Love KC). Emails with the author, December 28, 2018.

King, Mike (director, Youthfront). Interview with the author, August 24, 2017.

Lehleitner, Bob (pastor, Colonial Presbyterian Church). Interview with the author, October 27, 2017.

McElvain, Craig (executive director, Regional Evangelical Alliance of Churches). Interview with the author, June 23, 2017.

Steitz, Shanna (pastor, Community Christian Church). Interview with the author, June 20, 2017.

Online Resources

"Abolitionism," Encyclopedia Britannica Online, accessed Sept. 28, 2018, https://www.britannica.com/topic/abolitionism-European-and-American-social-movement.

"About KCPS," Kansas City Public Schools, accessed November 1, 2018, https://www.kcpublicschools.org/domain/98.

"About Us," Second Baptist Church, accessed Sept. 28, 2018, http://www.secondbaptistkcmo.com/About_Us.html.

"About Us," Shelterwood Residential Treatment Agency, accessed October 9, 2018, https://www.shelterwood.org/about-us/.

"And Then It Happened," Missouri Valley Special Collections, Kansas City Public Library, accessed October 18, 2018, http://www.kchistory.org/week-kansas-city-history/and-then-it-happened.

Benson, Arthur. "School Segregation and Desegregation in Kansas City." Accessed October 18, 2018, http://www.bensonlaw.com/kcmsd/deseg_history.htm.

Blake, Lee Ella. "The Great Exodus of 1879 and 1880 to Kansas." Kansas State College of Agriculture and Applied Science, Thesis, 1942, accessed Oct. 2, 2018, https://core.ac.uk/download/pdf/14342729.pdf.

Boxx, Rick. "Plain Talk." Integrity Moments, *One Place*, published August 6, 2010, https://www.oneplace.com/devotionals/integrity-moments-with-rick-boxx/integrity-moments-aug-6-2010-11635992.html.

"Caring For Kids," Citywide Prayer Movement KC, accessed October 15, 2018, https://www.citywideprayerkc.com/index.php?option=com_content&view=article&id=83&Itemid=480.

"Close Up: The Flood Of '77 – Part 4 of 4," KMBC-TV News 9, broadcasted September 16, 1977, published March 11, 2008, YouTube, https://www.youtube.com/watch?v=BphPu6xvIzI.

Coleman, Daniel. "Biography of Johnston Lykins (1800–1876), Missionary, Doctor, and Kansas City's Second Mayor." Missouri Valley Special Collections at the Kansas City Public Library, CD90, 2007. Accessed October 18, 2018, http://kchistory.org/content/

biography-johnston-lykins-1800-1876-missionary-doctor-and-kansas-citys-second-mayor.

Coleman, Daniel. "Biography of Samuel S. Mayerberg (1892–1964), Rabbi." Missouri Valley Special Collections, The Kansas City Public Library, 2007. http://www.kchistory.org/cdm4/item_viewer.php?CISOROOT=/Biographies&CISOPTR=245&CISOBOX=1&REC=2.

Coleman, Daniel. "Gabriel Prudhomme (1791–1831): Early Settler." Missouri Valley Special Collections, Kansas City Public Library, 2007. http://kcpl-vital-app.iii.com:9020/vital/access/services/Download/kcpl:18190/DOCUMENT?view=true&site_name=KC%20History.

Coleman, Daniel. "Samuel Mayerberg," The Kansas City Public Library, accessed November 14, 2018, https://pendergastkc.org/article/biography/samuel-mayerberg.

"Dan's Ride Through History." City Union Mission. YouTube, published April 3, 2013. https://www.youtube.com/watch?v=1Sn-4x0oGjY.

"David Rose: Special Effects Guru Talks About Godiva," CBN.com, accessed Feb. 6, 2018 http://www1.cbn.com/700club/david-rose-special-effects-guru-talks-about-godiva.

"Demographics," Blue Valley Schools, accessed November 1, 2018, https://district.bluevalleyk12.org/DistrictInformation/Pages/Demographics.aspx.

"The Extent of Fatherlessness," National Center for Fathering, accessed October 15, 2018, http://www.fathers.com/statistics-and-research/the-extent-of-fatherlessness/.

Fly, David K. "Reflections on the Kansas City Riot of 1968." Video Transcript, Missouri State Archives Presentation Videos, accessed October 17, 2018, https://www.sos.mo.gov/archives/presentations/ap_transcripts/kcriot.

Ford, Susan Jezak. "Napoleon W. Dible." The Kansas City Public Library, 1999, accessed November 16, 2018, https://pendergastkc.org/article/biography/napoleon-w-dible.

Garcia, J. Malcolm. "The Rev. David Altschul Is a Gift to One of the City's Iconic but Troubled Streets." *The Pitch*, Dec. 24, 2009. https://

www.pitch.com/news/article/20597601/the-rev-david-altschul-is-a-gift-to-one-of-the-citys-iconic-but-troubled-streets.

Harper, Kimberly, Stephanie Kukuljan, and John W. McKerley. "Thomas J. Pendergast (1872–1945)." State Historical Society of Missouri, accessed December 6, 2018, https://shsmo.org/historicmissourians/name/p/pendergast/.

"History of Calvary University," Calvary University, accessed Oct. 8, 2018, https://www.calvary.edu/history/.

"History of Lee's Summit," Lee's Summit, Mo. City Government, accessed October 26, 2018, http://cityofls.net/City-of-Lees-Summit/About-the-City/History.

"Holy Rosary Catholic Church Served by the Scalabrini Missionaries Since 1891," Holy Rosary Catholic Church, accessed December 17, 2018, https://www.hrkcmo.org/our-story.html.

Hutchinson, Bill. "What You Need to Know About the Assassination of Martin Luther King Jr." ABC News, April 2, 2018, https://abcnews.go.com/US/assassination-martin-luther-king-jr/story?id=54095424.

"Indian Removal Act," Primary Documents in American History, Library of Congress, accessed Sept. 27, 2018, https://www.loc.gov/rr/program/bib/ourdocs/indian.html.

Jackson, Sheldon. "English Quakers Tour Kansas in 1858." *The Kansas Historical Quarterly*, February 1944 (vol. 13 no. 1): 36-52, digitized by Kansas Historical Society, accessed October 26, 2018, https://www.kshs.org/p/english-quakers-tour-kansas-in-1858/12959.

Jezak Ford, Susan "Napoleon W. Dible," The Kansas City Public Library, 1999, accessed November 16, 2018, https://pendergastkc.org/article/biography/napoleon-w-dible.

"John Wornall and His Family," Wornall Majors House Museum, accessed November 2, 2018, http://www.wornallmajors.org/explore/wornall-house/john-wornall-his-family/.

"Kansas City History," City of Kansas City, MO. Accessed Sept. 27, 2018. http://kcmo.gov/Kansas-city-history/.

BIBLIOGRAPHY

"Kansas City Parks and Boulevard System," Kessler Society of Kansas City, http://www.georgekessler.org/index.php?option=com_content&view=section&id=8&Itemid=77.

"The Kansas-Nebraska Act," The History Place, 1996, accessed November 26, 2018, http://www.historyplace.com/lincoln/kansas.htm.

"Kansas Town Company Records, 1839–1957," The State Historical Society of Missouri Research Center-Kansas City, accessed October 23, 2018, https://shsmo.org/manuscripts/kansascity/k0352.pdf.

Keller, Timothy. "A Theology of Cities." Cru Press, 2012. https://www.cru.org/content/dam/cru/legacy/2012/02/A_Theology_of_Cities.pdf.

Keller, Timothy, *Why God Made Cities*. Redeemer City to City. Accessed Sept. 27, 2018. https://www.redeemercitytocity.com/ebook/.

Laney, Donald. "Life on Longview Farm." R. A. Long Historical Society, accessed October 26, 2018, http://ralonghistoricalsociety.org.

"Liberty Memorial," Historic American Buildings Survey, Architectural and Historical Research, LLC, accessed October 25, 2018, http://www.ahr-kc.com/reports/liberty_memorial/.

"Long's Legacy," R. A. Long Historical Society, accessed October 25, 2018. http://ralonghistoricalsociety.org/?fbclid=IwAR1o8caTWlSTkS2is96R2qchPfiU3w3-xL1JstYzMxDBUUJcBKqVmfW8w-I.

"Meet the Past: Annie Chambers," Kansas City PBS. Aired March 3, 2010. https://cove.kcpt.org/video/meet-the-past-annie-chambers/.

"Metro-Area Membership Report: Kansas City, MO-KS Metropolitan Statistical Area," The Association of Religion Data Archives, accessed Oct. 2, 2018, http://www.thearda.com/rcms2010/r/m/28140/rcms2010_28140_metro_name_2010.asp.

Milstead, Bertha Ellen. "Christian Missions Among the Kansas Indians." (master's thesis, Fort Hays State University, 1930), 199. https://scholars.fhsu.edu/theses/199.

"MLK at Western: Speech Transcription," Dr. Martin Luther King Jr., Western Michigan University Libraries, July 9, 2018, accessed Oct. 1, 2018, https://libguides.wmich.edu/mlkatwmu/speech.

"National Register of Historic Places Registration Form for Gillis Orphans Home," signed May 25, 2017, accessed Sept. 28, 2018, https://dnr.mo.gov/shpo/nps-nr/SG100001300.pdf.

"Our History," Independence Boulevard Christian Church, accessed October 25, 2018, http://ibcckc.org/history/.

"Our Story," Global Orphan Project, accessed October 16, 2018, https://goproject.org/learn/our-story/.

"Robert Alexander Long," Blue Skyways. Transcribed from *A Standard History of Kansas and Kansans*, (vol. 4) pp. 2007-2008. Compiled by William E. Connelley. Chicago: Lewis Publishing Company, 1918. https://web.archive.org/web/20130610042556/http://skyways.lib.ks.us/genweb/archives/1918ks/biol/longra.html.

Roe, Jason. "Exodusters Mark the Spot." Missouri Valley Special Collections, Kansas City Public Library, accessed October 18, 2018, http://www.kclibrary.org/blog/week-kansas-city-history/exodusters-mark-spot.

Roe, Jason. "In for the Landing." Missouri Valley Special Collections, accessed Sept. 27, 2018, http://www.kchistory.org/week-kansas-city-history/landing.

Roe, Jason. "Mess of a Massacre." Kansas City Public Library, Missouri Valley Special Collections, accessed November 29, 2018, http://www.kchistory.org/week-kansas-city-history/mess-massacre.

Saul, Norman E. "The Migration of the Russian-Germans to Kansas." *Kansas History: A Journal of the Central Plains*, 4 (vol. 40, no. 1, 1974) pp. 38-62. https://www.kshs.org/p/kansas-historical-quarterly-the-migration-of-the-russian-germans-to-kansas/13242.

"Secrets of Chambers," Missouri Valley Special Collections, Kansas City Public Library, accessed February 7, 2018, http://kchistory.org/week-kansas-city-history/secrets-chambers.

"Shawnee Indian Mission," Kansas State Historical Society, September 2013, https://www.kshs.org/kansapedia/shawnee-indian-mission/11913.

Skaptason, Bjorn. "Hobo Holiday! Pendergast Turkeys Fatten Goat Voters in Wake of Election!" Tom's Town Distilling Co. Accessed

November 14, 2018, https://www.toms-town.com/1939/12/hobo-holiday-pendergast-turkeys-fatten-goat-voters-in-wake-of-election/.

"State Ex Rel. Bluford v. Canada, 153 S.W.2d 12 (Mo. 1941)" Supreme Court of Missouri, Court Listener, accessed Oct. 6, 2018, https://www.courtlistener.com/opinion/3556344/state-ex-rel-bluford-v-canada/.

"Swope Park," KC Parks, accessed November 28, 2018, https://kcparks.org/places/swope-park/.

"Ten Years of Fighting Vice in Kansas City Missouri, Kansas City, MO." Society for Suppression of Commercialized Vice, 1923. Kansas City Public Library, Missouri Valley Special Collections accessed December 3, 2018, https://pendergastkc.org/collection/9130/mvsc-pf30674-s67t-1923/ten-years-fighting-vice-kansas-city-missouri.

Thackeray, Archibald. "Revival Artifacts ... Celebrating 'Times of Refreshing' (Acts 3:19)," Last modified December 27, 2009, https://revivalartifacts.blogspot.com/2010/04/charismatic-conference-at-arrowhead.html.

Trout, Carlynn. "Lucile H. Bluford." The State Historical Society of Missouri, accessed Oct. 6, 2018, https://shsmo.org/historicmissourians/name/b/bluford/.

"Vidy Metsker Tells How Youthfront Began." Youthfront. YouTube, published June 20, 2013, accessed December 6, 2018, https://www.youtube.com/watch?v=NAd_slXQ7Bw.

"Village Church History," Village Presbyterian Church, accessed November 5, 2018, https://www.villagepres.org/history--mission.html.

Walker, Edith. "Labor Problems During the First Year of Governor Martin's Administration." *Kansas History: A Journal of the Central Plains.* February 1936 (vol. 5, no. 1), pp. 33–53. Accessed January 23, 2019, https://www.kshs.org/p/labor-problems-during-the-first-year-of-governor-martin-s-administration/12671.

"We celebrated Our 153rd Church Anniversary in October 2016," Second Baptist Church, accessed December 14, 2018, http://secondbaptistchurchkc.com/wp-content/uploads/2016/08/SB-History-August-2016.pdf.

Welsh, Michael. "Building the Troost Wall: Structural Racism in Kansas City." Video, Anth 101: Anthropology for Everyone. Accessed Feb. 15, 2018, http://anth101.com/videos/.

Williamson, C., and M. Prior. Qtd. in "Commercial Sexual Exploitation: An Analysis of Prostitution in Kansas City." Alison Philips, UMKC Master's Thesis, 2017, accessed October 16, 2018, https://mospace.umsystem.edu/xmlui/bitstream/handle/10355/60582/Thesis_2017_Phillips.pdf?sequence=1&isAllowed=y.

About the Authors

Bill High is CEO of The Signatry: A Global Christian Foundation headquartered in Overland Park, Kansas. Prior to joining the foundation in 2000, Bill was a partner with Blackwell Sanders LLP, a national and international law firm. He is also the founder of iDonate, a fundraising software company serving the nonprofit community. Apart from writing books, Bill is a highly sought after speaker on topics relating to philanthropy and the transforming power of biblical generosity. He was named one of the Top 25 Philanthropy Speakers in the United States by Philanthropy Media.

Bill has been married to his wife Brooke for more than thirty years. They have four children, two sons-in-law, and two grandchildren.

Annika Bergen is director of communications for The Signatry. Prior to joining The Signatry, she served as a missionary in India and in Pittsburgh, Pennsylvania. She has volunteered with Exodus Cry to fight human trafficking, and she continues to write books and plant churches locally.

The Signatry
A Global Christian Foundation

The Signatry provides creative generosity solutions, including donor advised funds and complex asset giving, so donors can give more toward causes they are passionate about. The Signatry serves families by teaching a holistic view of legacy so they can live out values and impact the world. Learn more at thesignatry.com.

Engage Your Church
The Signatry offers multiple ways for your church to discover together the rich spiritual heritage of Kansas City.

- **Sermon Outlines** – Guide your church into Jesus's heart for the city as you teach them what He has done in Kansas City in the past. Inspire them that He can do the same again!

- **City Tours** – See Kansas City's history for yourself through a guided tour with The Signatry. As you travel to key historic spots, hear the little-known stories of the Christians who formed our city. Discover the real McCoy in Westport, view the river as Lewis and Clark first saw it, stand on the stones of the Liberty Memorial and hear about the Christian philanthropist who led its construction, and more.

Visit thesignatry.com/KCRoots to access these resources and more!

CPSIA information can be obtained
at www.ICGtesting.com
Printed in the USA
LVHW071051210719
624768LV00040B/1361/P